MEDIA
LITERACY
THINKING CRITICALLY ABOUT
NEWSPAPERS & MAGAZINES

Peyton Paxson

WALCH PUBLISHING

1   2   3   4   5   6   7   8   9   10

ISBN 0-8251-5499-5

Copyright © 2005
J. Weston Walch, Publisher
P.O. Box 658 • Portland, Maine 04104-0658
walch.com

Printed in the United States of America

Contents

Contents

From Magazine Publishers of America, "Teen Market Profile," 2004:

> With eight out of ten Teens reading magazines, this medium is one Teens depend upon to become informed . . . . In addition, Teens trust advertising in magazines the most—more than television, radio, or the Internet.

From *Editor and Publisher*, April 19, 2004:

> For the most part, and this should come as no surprise, teens don't really have an emotional attachment to newspapers. The NIE (Newspapers in Education) program does a good job covering elementary schools and college students but there's a gaping hole when it comes time to reaching teens in high schools.

This book, the seventh in a series on using media literacy to teach critical-thinking skills, focuses on two media with which teenagers have very different relationships. Magazines, targeted toward specific age groups and interests, are among teenagers' favorite sources of information. Newspapers, seeking a broader market, have little influence on teenagers; paradoxically, newspapers are arguably a more reliable source of accurate information than most magazines.

Contemporary discussions of print media commonly assume that the content delivery of newspapers and magazines will soon shift to electronic media. By most estimates, this shift will occur during the early adult years of students who are currently teenagers. As the mode of delivery changes, the content will also adapt. Nevertheless, people's need and desire for the types of information that newspapers and magazines currently provide will not decrease.

The units in this book provide students with information about newspapers and magazines as entertainment media, as businesses, and as sources of cultural exchange. The activities require students to describe this information and apply it in varied exercises. Students will analyze and evaluate how newspapers and magazines chronicle and shape their lives and the lives of others. They will encounter ethical considerations and economic issues. Students are also provided opportunities to develop their own creativity and ideas. Ultimately, this book strives to help students read critically both newspapers and magazines and to help them think critically about the events and ideas presented in these media.

CALVIN AND HOBBES ©1993 Watterson. Reprinted with permission of *UNIVERSAL PRESS SYNDICATE. All rights reserved.*

To the Student

IF YOU ARE LIKE MOST teenagers, you probably see newspapers and magazines as two very different media. There are far fewer teenage readers of newspapers than their publishers would like. However, many magazines successfully reach the teenage readers whom they are designed to attract. The definitions of newspapers and magazines are changing. Newspaper and magazine publishers realize that you and other readers will rely more on electronic sources of information in the future. Many observers believe that paper and ink versions of most newspapers and magazines will cease to exist during your lifetime. Although newspapers and magazines will survive, many will do so in electronic form.

It is important to study newspapers and magazines because they significantly affect the way we see our world and ourselves. The newspaper and magazine industries are constantly analyzing teenagers' habits, desires, and needs—they are trying to "get into your head." Therefore, it is important that teenagers investigate the newspaper and magazine industries.

There are probably several words in this book that you are not familiar with. You will find a glossary at the back of the book. Words that are defined in the glossary appear in bold type when first used in the book.

This book's purpose is to

- present you with methods for evaluating the content presented in today's newspapers and magazines

- encourage you to investigate your relationship with print media

- help you become more knowledgeable about the business of printing newspapers and magazines

The objectives of this unit are to help students

- appreciate the historical and cultural contexts of print media
- evaluate restrictions on freedom of speech
- understand that the presentation of information in print media is formulaic
- understand how publishers' social and economic agendas affect editorial decisions

THIS UNIT INTRODUCES students to the reasons why contemporary newspapers and magazines came into existence. The activities discuss many of the common practices used in print journalism to help students understand the narrative structure of newspapers and magazines. Students also learn that readers use newspapers and magazines for a variety of purposes, and that readers often selectively expose themselves to publications that support rather than challenge their viewpoints.

In this Unit . . .

The Anatomy of a Newspaper has students examine the presentation of information in newspapers and identify the different purposes newspapers serve.

The Forms of Magazines provides students with information about different categories of magazines. Questions require students to generate judgments about the reasons for conventional publishing practices.

Who Reads What? involves students in a discussion of newspapers with an older adult, preferably a senior citizen. Students then compare how teenagers and older adults receive information from newspapers.

The First Amendment asks students how society should balance freedom of the press with ethical responsibilities.

Ladies' Home Journal provides historical information about that magazine's appeal to young women a century ago. Students evaluate the role played by parents and other older adults in the lives of teens today and investigate whether magazines provide substitutes for this role.

Keep It Simple! introduces students to readability indexes and has students evaluate the efforts by print journalists to simplify their writing. Students then identify words that are unknown to them in a newspaper, find dictionary definitions for those words, and suggest better words.

Where in the World? asks students to consider how newspapers portray the conditions of other nations. Students read a daily newspaper and identify a nation of which they know little or nothing and conduct independent research to learn more about the nation in question. They are then asked to provide qualitative opinions about that nation.

THE PUBLICATION OF NEWSPAPERS in America began in early colonial times. *The Boston News-Letter,* the first regularly published American newspaper, began in 1704. Hundreds of newspapers have come and gone since then. A major challenge for the first American newspapers was profitability. In the early days of the United States, there were few advertisers. This is because there were few branded products. Newspapers relied instead on **circulation** (readership) for most of their income, yet many Americans could not read, or they could not afford a newspaper. Most American communities were also too small to support a successful newspaper. This began to change in the mid-nineteenth century. The trend toward taxpayer-supported public education helped more people learn to read, and industrialization brought a tremendous increase in branded goods and advertising. The United States Civil War, which took place from 1861 to 1865 and affected nearly every American family during that time, generated great public demand for news from Washington and from the battlefield. In fact, until the Civil War, many daily newspapers had not bothered to publish a Sunday edition.

> **A major challenge for the first American newspapers was profitability.**

In the late nineteenth century, cities began to experience tremendous population growth. Men and women from rural farm areas moved to the cities in search of work in the new factories that were rising in and around cities. Cities also grew with the arrival of thousands of European and Asian immigrants seeking better opportunities in the United States.

Two of the most famous newspaper publishers at this time were Joseph Pulitzer and William Randolph Hearst. Pulitzer's *World* and Hearst's *Journal* competed against each other for readers in New York City by increasingly relying on **sensationalism** in their reporting. Historians refer to this period of often-inaccurate news and attention-getting gimmicks as the era of "Yellow Journalism." The term came from a popular comic strip of the time, "The Yellow Kid." Both publishers began to rely more heavily on earning money from advertisers rather than from sales to readers. Hearst even dropped the price of the *Journal* to a penny. The tactics of Pulitzer and Hearst proved successful. Both publishers increased their circulations from thousands of readers to hundreds of thousands, and they earned millions of dollars from advertisers.

The most shameful episode involving the two newspapers occurred in 1898. An American battleship, the *U.S.S. Maine,* exploded in the harbor of Havana, Cuba. At the time, Spain controlled Cuba. The cause of the explosion has never been satisfactorily explained. However, the *World* and the *Journal* published articles that encouraged the United States to declare war against Spain. Both Pulitzer and Hearst knew that some of their articles exaggerated the facts or contained outright lies. Although the Spanish-American War only lasted a few months and the United States won, the reasons for the war remain suspect.

The twentieth century brought more changes to the newspaper industry. Many owners of

(continued)

individual newspapers sold them to large corporations. By 2004, approximately ten companies owned most of the large daily newspapers in the United States. Technology also brought changes to the industry. Commercial radio, which arose in the 1920s, and television, which arrived in the late 1940s, began to compete with newspapers for advertisers' money. Printing advances brought the use of color photography and graphics to newspapers. Electronic media, including the Internet, changed the way that the public thought about the timeliness of news. The expression "that's as old as yesterday's news" became "that's so fifteen minutes ago." As a result, many newspapers created web sites to provide more timely information to the public.

Magazines

Magazines became popular at about the same time as newspapers, and for some of the same reasons. The United States' railroads integrated their rail systems in the 1870s. This meant that manufacturers of goods could ship their products throughout the nation. Mass manufacturing and mass distribution of products created a demand for mass marketing (and vice versa). Because industrial technology allowed manufacturers to make millions of items every day, manufacturers had to sell millions of items every day. In an age before radio and television, print media provided advertisers with their best opportunity to promote their products. Seeking advertisers' dollars, American publishers started over seven thousand magazines between 1885 and 1905. Many of these magazines quickly failed. But between 1890 and 1905, monthly magazine circulation rose from 18 million to 64 million; weekly magazine circulation rose from 28 million to 36 million.

Many magazines in the past century were general-interest magazines, aimed at a large audience. However, as we will discuss in Unit 3, when radio and television began to grow in popularity, magazines began to seek out *niches,* or smaller segments of readers. This trend continues today. While some general-interest magazines are still popular, hundreds of magazines appeal to specific **demographic** and **psychographic** groups. Demographics are statistics about people grouped by such information as age, gender, ethnicity, geography, and income. For example, we know the demographic group that is most likely to read *Cosmopolitan* is women. Psychographics identify people by their interests, attitudes, values, and habits (including buying habits). For example, the psychographic group that is most likely to read *American Hunter* is people interested in guns and hunting.

Print Production

The production of a newspaper or magazine can be a complex process involving hundreds or even thousands of people. Publishers are the people responsible for the business decisions that affect newspapers and magazines. Editors are responsible for the editorial content (articles and stories) of each newspaper and magazine. Often, different editors supervise different sections of a publication. For example, a daily newspaper will usually have a sports editor, a front-page editor, and so forth. The editor-in-chief is the person who supervises the activity of each editor. Editorial content, including news stories, **feature stories,** and other text, comes from several types of writers. Some writers may be permanent employees of the publication who receive a regular salary. Other writers may be correspondents, who are

(continued)

Newspapers and Magazines Buzz

regular contributors to a publication but are paid for each story that is accepted by the publication. Some newspapers and magazines accept unsolicited stories. In these cases, writers submit their work to publications and ask for it to be published.

Other people involved in the newspaper and magazine industry include sales staff who sell advertising "space" (pages or parts of a page) to advertisers. The circulation department works to add subscribers, distribute the publication to subscribers and newsstands, and respond to any problems subscribers have in receiving the publication. Finally, the production and printing of publications often require a large staff of highly skilled people.

The Anatomy of a Newspaper -

DAILY NEWSPAPERS in the United States tend to have the same arrangement of information, regardless of where you live. The front page contains the news that the newspaper's editors think is most interesting to their readers. The news articles, also called news stories, may be local, regional, national, or international. Each article begins with a headline at the top. The headline gives the reader a general idea of the main topic of the article. The editors of the newspaper place the most important article at the top of the front page using the headline to generate readers' interest and help sell copies of that newspaper at a newsstand.

Answer the following questions. Use another sheet of paper, if necessary.

1. Newspaper editors refer to information that appears on the top half of a newspaper page as "above the fold." People who design Internet web pages also use this term. Do an Internet search using a search engine such as Google (www.google.com) or Dogpile (www.dogpile.com) placing the term "above the fold" within quotation marks. Explain what web designers mean by the expression "above the fold."

If an article comes from a **news service,** the article will usually state that. If the article was written by a local reporter (or several reporters) the article will have a *byline* listing the writer's name (or the writers' names) below the article's headline. Newspapers write articles in an *inverted pyramid* style. This means that the beginning of the article contains most of the important information, with the rest of the article providing additional details.

2. Explain why you think newspaper articles provide the most important information at the beginning of each article.

Look through the first three or four pages of today's newspaper.

3. What do the editors of the newspaper think was the most important news story today? Explain how you know this.

4. Looking at some of the other articles on the first few pages of the newspaper, do you agree with the editors that this was the most important news of the day? Explain why or why not.

(continued)

The Anatomy of a Newspaper -------------------------

Daily newspapers are exactly that—newspapers that appear every day. On some days there is more news to report than on others.

 5. What do you think a newspaper's editors do when there is little or no important news to report? Explain your answer.

Most daily newspapers once had a section called the Women's section. This section typically contained personal advice columns, gossip about local and national celebrities, and feature stories, rather than "hard" news. Within the past twenty to thirty years, newspapers changed the name of the Women's section. Today, they call this section "Living," "Life," or "Lifestyle."

 6. Explain what you think happened in society to cause newspapers to change the name of the Women's section.

As mentioned in the Buzz for this unit, newspaper publishers rely on advertisers to generate profit. Newspapers contain several types of advertisements. *Display advertisements* appear next to editorial content. Advertisers pay for these advertisements based on "space," or size—the larger the advertisement, the more expensive it is for the advertiser. If advertisers want to use colored ink, they pay an additional charge for that. Advertisers receive *volume discounts*—the more advertising they buy over a period of time, the lower the price they pay for each advertisement.

 7. Explain why you think newspapers offer volume discounts to advertisers.

Other advertisements appear in the "classified advertising" section of the newspapers. The term comes from the fact that these advertisements are organized by subject matter. For example, classified advertisements contain an automobile section, perhaps organized by brand of car. There may also be classified advertisements for pets for sale, real estate, antiques, and any other item or service that can be sold.

The third common type of newspaper advertisement is the flyer. This term comes from the fact that these inserted advertisements tend to fly out of the newspaper when it is opened by the reader. Today, flyers are often printed with full-color photography on glossy paper. Most flyers appear in the Sunday edition of daily newspapers.

(continued)

The Anatomy of a Newspaper -------------------------

8. Explain why you think flyers are most likely to be included in the Sunday edition of a daily newspaper.

In many communities, the Thursday edition of a newspaper includes an additional section—called a *supplement*—devoted to the arts (museums, music, and theater). The Thursday supplement also contains reviews of movies and local restaurants.

9. Explain why you think the arts and entertainment section usually appears in the Thursday edition of daily newspapers.

Daily newspapers appear in one of two formats. Most are broadsheets, with long pages that are folded and creased lengthwise, and then folded over again for sale or carrying. The other, less common format is the tabloid. These newspapers are closer in size to magazines and are only folded lengthwise. Examples of tabloid newspapers include the *Chicago Sun-Times,* the *New York Post,* and Denver's *Rocky Mountain News.* (These are not to be confused with supermarket tabloids, which are discussed in Unit 3.) Most tabloid newspapers in the United States appear in large cities where there is more than one daily newspaper. Besides looking different, the two types of newspapers tend to be very different in how they present information.

You probably already know that people practice selective exposure. When discussing publishing, this means that readers will choose to read things that they find interesting and agreeable. Thus, a teenage male may glance at the headlines on the front page of the newspaper, read the sports

(continued)

The Anatomy of a Newspaper -

section, and completely ignore the "Living" section. Similarly, a person who favors the Republican party will tend to read newspapers that promote the Republican party's political agenda.

Publishers of tabloid newspapers design them to appeal to a certain type of reader. It would be foolish to believe that all a newspaper does is present facts. Facts are subject to interpretation. (Is the glass half empty or half full?) Some facts can be emphasized, while other facts can be downplayed or not printed at all. Besides presenting news articles, newspapers also offer essays by writers called *columnists* (called this because they usually write essays designed to fit within one column of the newspaper). Newspaper columnists are supposed to interpret events based on their personal opinions.

Consider the following information:

- Tabloid newspapers rely heavily on newsstand (single copy) sales rather than subscription sales; broadsheets rely on subscription sales.
- Tabloid newspapers emphasize state lotteries more than broadsides do.
- Tabloid newspapers emphasize local stories more than national and international news; competing broadsheets tend to emphasize national and international news.
- Many people criticize tabloid newspapers for using sensationalism in their reporting.

Based on this information, answer each of the following questions.

10. Who do you think is more likely to read a tabloid than a broadsheet when given a choice—a college graduate or a person who is not a college graduate? Explain your answer.

11. Who do you think is more likely to read a tabloid than a broadsheet—a person who watches a lot of television, or a person who watches very little television? Explain your answer.

12. There are fewer daily newspapers today than there were ten years ago. In particular, there are very few tabloid-style daily newspapers still published today. Explain what you think is happening in the world and in the media industry that has hurt the popularity of tabloid newspapers.

The Forms of Magazines -

WHILE DAILY NEWSPAPERS tend to have a common format, magazines are not always organized in the same way. This is because different magazines serve the needs of different readers. You are probably most familiar with "consumer" magazines. These magazines appeal to readers based on their interests, hobbies, and lifestyles. You may be less familiar with "trade" or "professional" magazines. These publications are directed toward people in specific types of occupations. Trade and professional magazines are often important sources of information that help people become and remain successful in their type of work.

Answer the following questions. Use another sheet of paper, if necessary.

1. Do you think the number of trade and professional magazines in the future will increase, stay the same, or decrease? Explain your answer.

2. The Internal Revenue Service allows taxpayers to deduct the cost of certain business expenses from their income. For example, a businessperson may be able to deduct the cost of a new computer from the income on which she has to pay taxes. Similarly, a mechanic can deduct the price of tools that he needs for his work.

   Do you think that people should be able to deduct the cost of subscribing to trade and professional magazines from their taxable income? Explain why or why not.

A third important type of magazine is the scholarly journal. These magazines contain articles written by college professors, schoolteachers, and researchers. They contain few, if any, advertisements. The most prestigious of these journals are "refereed," which means that a panel of experts decides whether an article should be published. Those colleges that consider themselves "research universities" require their professors to publish a certain number of articles in these journals in order to keep their jobs. (Thus, the phrase, "publish or perish.")

3. Explain why you think some colleges require their professors to publish articles in scholarly journals.

Editors of consumer magazines very carefully select the photographs they place on the cover of their magazines. For example, the editors of *People* magazine keep track of which celebrities' photographs seem to help sell copies of the magazine.

(continued)

The Forms of Magazines -------------------------

4. Imagine that the editors of *People* magazine have put you in charge of selecting which celebrities to place on its cover this week. List three celebrities and explain why each would be a good choice to help sell magazines this week.

  •

  •

  •

Some magazines rely more heavily on single-copy sales at newsstands, while others rely more heavily on mail subscriptions.

5. Describe what types of magazines probably rely more on newsstand sales than on subscription sales. Explain why you think this is so.

6. Describe what types of magazines you think rely more on subscription sales than single-copy sales. Explain why you think this is so.

7. Magazines that rely mostly on subscriptions tend to have an easily found table of contents toward the front of the magazine. This table of contents tells readers where they can find different articles or sections of the magazine. Magazines that rely on newsstand sales may or may not have tables of contents, and if they do, the table of contents is usually harder to find.

   Explain why you think magazines that rely on newsstand sales make it relatively difficult to find their tables of contents.

(continued)

The Forms of Magazines -

The length of a magazine subscription can vary, depending on how often a magazine is published. Some magazines are published weekly, some monthly, and some (including most scholarly journals) are published quarterly, or four times a year.

8. Explain why you think most sports magazines are published weekly rather than monthly.

9. Explain why you think most scholarly journals are published quarterly.

10. Consumer magazines rely heavily on advertising for their profits. During which season of the year do you think consumer magazines contain the most advertisements? Explain why.

Who Reads What? -

THE INTRODUCTION to this book mentioned the fact that teenagers do not read newspapers as often as publishers would like. Publishers want to attract teenage readers for a number of reasons. One reason is that there are so many teenagers in the United States—about 32 million in the early 2000s, out of a total population of about 284 million Americans. Another reason is that teenagers spent an estimated $112.5 billion in 2003. That makes teenagers attractive to companies that advertise in newspapers and magazines. Teenagers read a wide variety of magazines, many of which are specifically targeted to teenagers. However, less than half of American teenagers read the newspaper on a daily basis. This often changes as teenagers age. Studies have shown that the older a person is, the more likely she or he is to read newspapers regularly.

Answer the following questions. Use another sheet of paper, if necessary.

1. Why do you think older adults are more likely to read newspapers than teenagers are?

Teenagers tend to be a more attractive **target market** for advertisers than senior citizens, even though many seniors have more money to spend on advertised products.

2. Discuss this fact with an older adult, preferably a senior citizen. Ask that older adult why he or she thinks teenagers are more attractive to advertisers than senior citizens are. Then write a summary of your discussion.

3. Do you agree with that older adult? Explain why or why not.

4. Look through a newspaper and identify three articles (not advertisements) that you find interesting. Provide a brief description of each article.

   Article 1
   Headline:

   Brief description of what article is about:

   Why this article is interesting to you:

(continued)

Who Reads What? -----------------------------

Article 2
Headline:

Brief description of what article is about:

Why this article is interesting to you:

Article 3
Headline:

Brief description of what article is about:

Why this article is interesting to you:

5. Look through the same newspaper you used for question 4 and find three advertisements (not articles) that you find interesting. Provide a brief description of each advertisement.

Advertisement 1
Product or service being advertised:

Why this advertisement is interesting to you:

Advertisement 2
Product or service being advertised:

Why this advertisement is interesting to you:

Advertisement 3
Product or service being advertised:

Why this advertisement is interesting to you:

(continued)

Who Reads What? --------------------------------

6. Now ask an older adult, preferably a senior citizen, to look through the same newspaper and identify three articles (not advertisements) that she or he finds interesting. Provide a brief description of each article.

   Article 1
   Headline:

   Brief description of what article is about:

   Why this article is interesting to older adult:

   Article 2
   Headline:

   Brief description of what article is about:

   Why this article is interesting to older adult:

   Article 3
   Headline:

   Brief description of what article is about:

   Why this article is interesting to older adult:

7. Ask the same older adult to look through the same newspaper and find three advertisements (not articles) that she or he finds interesting. Provide a brief description of each advertisement.

   Advertisement 1
   Product or service being advertised:

   Why this advertisement is interesting to the older adult:

(continued)

Who Reads What? -

Advertisement 2

Product or service being advertised:

Why this advertisement is interesting to the older adult:

Advertisement 3

Product or service being advertised:

Why this advertisement is interesting to the older adult:

8. Compare your answers to question 4 and the answers the older adult provided you in question 6. What similarities and differences did you find? Explain your answer.

9. Compare your answers to question 5 and the answers the older adult provided you in question 7. What similarities and differences did you find? Explain your answer.

10. Imagine that after you have completed the questions above, a newspaper editor asks you for advice on how to attract more teenage readers. Based on the research you conducted here, what would you tell the newspaper editor?

The First Amendment —

THE FIRST AMENDMENT to the United States Constitution, ratified in 1791, reads as follows:

> Congress shall make no law respecting an establishment of religion, or prohibiting the free exercise thereof; or abridging the freedom of speech or of the press; or the right of the people peaceably to assemble, and to petition the government for a redress of grievances.

"Abridging the freedom of speech or of the press" means limiting or reducing freedom of speech and the press.

Answer the following questions. Use another sheet of paper, if necessary.

1. If we take the First Amendment at face value, it prohibits *any* limits on the press. Do you think that courts today would refuse to allow the government to place limits on the press, no matter the situation? Explain your answer.

2. Do you think that a newspaper should be able to print anything its publisher and editor want to publish? Explain why or why not.

3. Do you think that a newspaper should be able to publish an embarrassing (but true) story about the private life of a famous person? Explain why or why not.

(continued)

The First Amendment -

4. Do you think that a newspaper should be able to publish an embarrassing (*and false*) story about the private life of a famous person? Explain why or why not.

Suppose that a famous person has died. A newspaper prints an article claiming that the famous person committed several serious crimes when she was alive. The article is false. Obviously, the dead person cannot defend herself, and, in this case, she left no family members or close friends.

5. Should the newspaper be punished for printing the false story? Explain why or why not.

6. Regardless of how you answered question 5, if the newspaper were to be punished, who should seek that punishment? Explain your answer.

7. Regardless of how you answered question 5, if the newspaper were to be punished, what do you think most people would see as the best punishment? Explain your answer.

Ladies' Home Journal -

AS MENTIONED in the Buzz for this unit, the period during the late 1800s and the early 1900s was the age of American urbanization. During this time, many Americans moved from rural areas (farms) to urban areas (cities). They did so to search for work in the new factories that arose in and near cities. In addition, many new Americans arrived from other countries as immigrants in search of a better life. Of course, many of the newcomers to the cities were females. Before young women moved away from home, they often relied on their mothers for information. This included information about women's traditional roles at that time, including cooking, keeping a house, and raising children. When these young women moved, many of them sought new sources of information on these topics.

Curtis Publishing Company first published *Ladies' Home Journal* in 1883. In 1889, Edward Bok became the magazine's editor. He remained with the magazine for twenty years. As editor, Bok understood the role his magazine played for its readers. He realized "that in thousands of cases the American mother was not the confidante of her daughter, and reasoned if an inviting human personality could be created on the printed page that would supply this lamentable [sad] lack of American family life, girls would flock to such a figure."[1] Bok did not claim to be an expert on women's issues. Rather than write about these issues himself, he hired other people, usually women, to write about the issues that were important to female readers.

Answer the following questions. Use another sheet of paper, if necessary.

1. Bok uses the word *confidante.* Explain what a confidante is. (If you are not sure, look the word up in a dictionary, then describe it in your own words.)

---

[1] Bok, Edward, *The Americanization of Edward Bok; An Autobiography* (New York: Scribner's 1924), p. 169.

(continued)

Ladies' Home Journal -

2. Do you have a confidante? Explain your answer.

3. Do you think most teenage females feel that their mother or some other older female is their confidante? Explain why or why not.

4. Do you think most teenage males feel that their father or some other older male is their confidante? Explain why or why not.

5. Can a parent or an older adult of the opposite sex be a teenager's confidante? Explain why or why not.

Because Bok found that many young women in the early 1900s did not confide in their mothers, he tried to have his magazine serve as a substitute for "motherly advice."

6. Do you believe that today's teenage females look to magazines for "motherly advice"? Explain why or why not.

7. Do you believe that today's teenage males look to magazines for "fatherly advice"? Explain why or why not.

Keep It Simple! -

AS DISCUSSED in the Buzz for this unit, magazines and newspapers became popular in the late nineteenth century, when many more people had learned to read. However, magazines and newspapers are still careful today about making sure that their articles and stories are easy to read. Readability factors include the layout of a page. For example, writing that is too small is hard to read (it makes the reader tired). In addition, publications have found that dividing stories into columns makes reading a page of text easier. Also important are such considerations as the length of sentences, the length of paragraphs, and the average number of syllables in words, which affect the ease or difficulty of reading a publication.

Two of the most commonly used readability tests are the Fog Index and the Flesch-Kincaid Index. Both indexes try to determine how much school a reader would have had to complete to understand an article or story. The indexes are shown in the box below.

The Fog Index

Reading Level (Grade) = (average number of words in sentences divided by the percentage of words of three or more syllables) × 0.4

(*The New York Times* has an average Fog Index of 11 – 12. *Time* magazine has an average Fog index of 11.)

The Flesch-Kincaid Index

Reading Level (Grade) = (0.39 × average number of words in sentences + 11.8 × average number of syllables per word – 15.59)

Robert Gunning, who created the Fog Index, and Rudolph Flesch served as consultants to newspapers and news services in the 1940s and 1950s. They helped newspapers and news services develop articles and stories that were easier to read. Gunning told newspaper reporters, "Write as you talk . . . . Why should a police reporter say an accident victim suffered 'contusions and abrasions' when he really means 'cuts and bruises?'"[2] In 1952, Gunning claimed that he had been able to help the newspapers for which he worked to lower their average reading level from eleventh grade to ninth grade.

---

[2] "The Unreadable Press," *Time,* 3 March 1947, p. 71.

(continued)

Keep It Simple! -

Answer the following questions. Use another sheet of paper, if necessary.

1. Think about a daily newspaper that is available in your community. Is it a good idea or a bad idea that a reader who has not completed high school can read that newspaper successfully? Explain your answer.

When Gunning and Flesch first began working with newspapers, many newspaper editors and writers complained that they were being asked to "dumb down" their articles and stories.

2. Explain what the term "dumb down" means to you.

3. What is one benefit of "dumbing down" a newspaper article? Explain your answer.

4. What is one problem with "dumbing down" a newspaper article? Explain your answer.

(continued)

Keep It Simple! -

5. Let's examine how successful newspaper editors are in making their newspapers easy to read. Look through a newspaper and find three words that you don't know or aren't sure of. List them in the chart. Then look up each word in a dictionary and write the definition next to each word.

unknown word	dictionary definition

6. For each word you chose above, suggest a simpler word and explain why your word is better.

newspaper's word	your word	why your word is better

Where in the World? -

MOST DAILY NEWSPAPERS focus on events that occur in the communities where they are published. However, they will also include important news about events that occur in your state, in your nation, and throughout the world. Where these stories appear in your daily newspaper depends on the editor's opinion about what is important to readers. Some newspapers focus much more on local and regional events than do other newspapers, based on what type of reader reads each newspaper.

Answer the following questions. Use another sheet of paper, if necessary.

1. Think about the people in your community. Which groups of people in your community would be more interested in articles about local events than they would be about international events? Explain your answer.

2. Again, think about the people in your community. Which groups of people in your community would be more interested in articles about International events than other readers would be? Explain your answer.

3. Without first checking the newspaper for help, think about what is going on in the world today. Then identify at least one foreign nation whose current events interest (or should interest) you. Explain why.

(continued)

Where in the World? -

4. Now look through a newspaper and find an article about a foreign nation of which you know little or nothing.

   • List that nation's name here:

   Using library or Internet resources, learn more about that nation and fill in the following information:

   • Where nation is located:

   • Land area (size):

   • Population:

   • Major language(s):

   • Major religion(s):

   • Gross Domestic Product (GDP), also known as
     Gross National Product (GNP):

   • Literacy rate:

   • Infant mortality rate:

   Now fill in the same information about the United States:

   • Land area (size):

   • Population:

   • Major language(s):

   • Major religion(s):

   • Gross Domestic Product (GDP), also known as
     Gross National Product (GNP):

   • Literacy rate:

   • Infant mortality rate:

(continued)

Where in the World? -

Referring to the same nation that you studied in question 4, answer the following questions. (If you need more information to answer these questions, do more research!)

5. Compared to the United States, would you describe this nation as a rich nation, a poor nation, or in between? Explain your answer.

6. Compared to the United States, would you describe this nation as a peaceful nation or a nation that is not peaceful? Explain your answer.

7. Would you describe this nation as one in which most of its citizens are usually happy, usually unhappy, or in between? Explain your answer.

8. Would you describe this nation as an ally (friend) of the United States, an enemy of the United States, or in between? Explain your answer.

9. Is this nation one that American newspaper readers need to keep informed about? Explain why or why not.

The objectives of this unit are to help students

- understand the rights and responsibilities of a free press
- identify the competing social, economic, and political interests that newspapers serve
- understand the need to balance the competing interests affected by newspaper coverage (or lack of coverage)
- assess the newsworthiness of specific people and events

AS DISCUSSED in the introduction to this book, teenagers are infrequent readers of newspapers. Newspaper readership tends to increase with age, as older readers seek additional information about social, economic, and political issues with which to make informed decisions about life's increasing responsibilities. This unit focuses on newspaper content that appeals to teenagers today to help students develop critical-thinking skills about what information newspapers present and how they present it.

In this Unit . . .

Scandals presents students with information about a real-life political scandal and asks students to evaluate the impact of such scandals as well as the ethics of publicizing them.

The Op-Ed Page has students investigate the role of newspapers in building and maintaining public sentiment about important social, economic, and political issues.

Silence! provides students with the opportunity to examine how economic considerations determine which events and issues newspapers will discuss and which they will not.

Newsmakers asks students to review recent events and identify those persons who are the most notable for a particular week and for the year in general.

Headlines is a group activity that provides students with the opportunity to test and develop their reading and comprehension skills. Students read several news articles and then create their own headlines for each article.

To Show or Not to Show? uses the controversies surrounding the photographs of prisoners being tortured by American soldiers at Iraq's Abu Ghraib prison and the photographs of soldiers' caskets returning from Iraq as the focus of an exercise in which students evaluate the responsibilities of the press during wartime.

Crime and Newspapers requires students to balance the interests of the accused, the victim, and the press in the reporting of a crime.

SUPPOSE THAT Britney Spears trips and falls walking out of a Victoria's Secret store one day, and a photographer who is present takes a photograph of the fall. We know that the purpose of newspapers is to provide news. But what *is* news? Newspaper editors understand that news is whatever helps sell newspapers. Each of us decides individually whether we care if Britney fell and slightly bruised her knee. Newspaper editors know that enough of us do care, and many newspapers will print the photograph. Meanwhile, if a flood in a nation that few of us have heard of kills fifty people, the story may be reported in an article of only two or three sentences. This brief story may then be "buried" deep inside the newspaper.

> **Newspaper editors understand that news is whatever helps sell newspapers.**

We have already been taught that the basic facts are "who, what, when, where, why, and how." However, newspaper editors must first decide whether to send a reporter out to cover an event and gather these facts. If a reporter covers an event, the "why" and "how" of the event are subject to the reporter's personal interpretation. When the reporter writes the article, newspaper editors then decide how much emphasis to give to that article.

Newspaper editors make decisions every day about what is news and what is not news. They frequently conduct research about their readers to learn what readers consider important. Newspapers also study how we want news to be reported. Recent research indicates that we want our news provided in shorter articles than before. Readers also like lots of charts and graphs, and we want key points of information in a newspaper article highlighted.

As discussed in Unit 1, newspapers serve two different groups of people: readers and advertisers. If a newspaper fails to please its readers, the circulation will drop. Advertisers will then be less willing to place advertisements in that newspaper. Therefore, newspapers publish the types of content that they believe will attract and maintain circulation. Newspapers are also aware that certain types of news may make advertisers unhappy. If an advertiser believes that a newspaper is publishing stories that are unfavorable to that advertiser, it may reduce or discontinue its advertising in that newspaper. This consideration also affects newspapers' decisions about what is news and how they report it.

Scandals -

IT IS COMMON KNOWLEDGE that scandals help to sell newspapers.

Answer the following questions. Use another sheet of paper, if necessary.

1. In your own words, describe what a "scandal" is.

2. Why do scandals help to sell newspapers? Explain your answer.

Jack Ryan was a Republican candidate for the United States Senate representing Illinois. In June 2004, the *Chicago Tribune* sued in California to gain access to Ryan's divorce records there. Ryan had been married to the actor Jeri Lynn Ryan, who has appeared in television's *Boston Public* and *Star Trek: Voyager*. In those divorce records, Jeri Ryan claimed, among other things, that her husband had forced her to go to kinky sex clubs against her will. When the *Chicago Tribune* sued for the divorce records, both Jack Ryan and Jeri Ryan asked that the records be kept secret. However, the court ruled in favor of the media, and the Ryans' divorce records were released.

3. What would be a good reason to publish this information?

4. What would be a good reason not to publish this information?

(continued)

Scandals –

5. The Ryans had a son who was nine years old at the time of this controversy. Should newspapers have considered this when deciding whether to publish information from the Ryans' divorce records? Explain why or why not.

6. Many people observed that although Jeri Ryan made the accusations about her husband in papers filed in court, those accusations were never actually proved. Should this have made a difference to newspaper editors when deciding whether to publish information from the Ryans' divorce records? Explain why or why not.

7. Do you think that the average newspaper reader cares about the family lives of political candidates? Explain why or why not.

A couple of days after the Chicago media released the Ryans' divorce records, Jack Ryan withdrew from the race. Ryan said that the media were "out of control" and claimed that the actions of the *Chicago Tribune* were "truly outrageous."

8. Do you agree with Ryan? Explain why or why not.

The Op-Ed Page -

"OP-ED" IS SHORT for *opinion-editorial.* The Op-Ed section of a newspaper typically contains political cartoons, a selection of letters to the newspaper from its readers, and one or more editorial articles. Most newspaper editors attempt to keep their opinions out of the news sections of their newspapers. However, the Op-Ed section provides readers with the opinions of that newspaper's management on important events of the day. For example, an editorial may promote or oppose a political decision that affects the newspaper's community. Before political elections, many newspapers endorse candidates and ask their readers to vote for those candidates. They may also discuss the reasons for their opposition to other candidates.

As discussed in the Buzz in Unit 1, there were many more newspapers in the past than there are today. In the early to mid-twentieth century, many communities had at least two newspapers. It was common then to have one newspaper that generally favored the Democratic party and another newspaper that generally favored the Republican party. Thus, the viewpoint of the nation's two major political parties were usually presented to a community's readers. Today, however, only the largest communities in the United States have more than one daily newspaper.

Answer the following questions. Use another sheet of paper, if necessary.

1. Talk to an older adult who is a regular voter. Ask him or her whether a newspaper's endorsement of a political candidate has ever played a part in that person's decision for whom they would vote. Write his or her answer below.

   Ask the older adult to explain his or her answer, and write the answer below.

2. If you were uncertain about whom to vote for in an upcoming political election, would you consult your local daily newspaper's endorsements of political candidates to help you make a decision? Explain why or why not.

3. Regardless of whether a newspaper favors a particular candidate, do you think that a newspaper has a duty to present information to its readers on the views and ideas of all candidates for political office? Explain why or why not.

(continued)

The Op-Ed Page -

Imagine that you are a newspaper editor. A large company is considering whether or not to build a new store in your community. This new store will employ many local workers. However, many people worry that this big company will force several smaller stores to close. This is because these smaller stores, which are locally owned, will not be able to sell merchandise as inexpensively as the big new store.

4. What would be a good reason to write an editorial supporting the new store? Explain your answer.

5. What would be a good reason to write an editorial opposing the new store? Explain your answer.

6. Do you believe the new store's arrival in your community would be a good thing? Explain why or why not.

Imagine that you are a newspaper editor. Your community is debating whether to allow gay couples to get married in city hall. Opinion polls show that the community is equally divided on the issue. Approximately half of the people asked say they support gay marriage. The other half says it opposes gay marriage.

7. Regardless of your personal opinion on gay marriage, do you think that it would be a good idea for your newspaper to publish an editorial about the issue? Explain why or why not.

Silence!- -

IT HAS BEEN SAID that freedom of speech is equal to freedom not to speak. For example, it is unconstitutional to make someone recite the Pledge of Allegiance. If somebody does not want to say the pledge, that person cannot be made to do so. Similarly, newspapers and magazines have constitutional rights not to speak. This means that if an advertiser wants to place an advertisement in a newspaper or magazine, the publication does not have to accept and print the advertisement. The publication's owners might disagree with the message in the advertisement, or they might view the advertisement as dishonest or offensive to readers.

Although there are thousands of different magazines in the world, chances are that your community has one or two daily newspapers at the most. This means that if a newspaper refuses to run a person's advertisement, the message of the advertisement may go unheard.

Suppose that StinkCo wants to build a smelly, smoky factory next to a residential neighborhood. People in the neighborhood try to place an advertisement in the local newspaper. This advertisement describes the reasons why those people do not want StinkCo to build the factory. Those reasons are too complicated to be effectively communicated in a radio or television advertisement. However, the local newspaper (the only one in that community) refuses to run the advertisement.

Answer the following questions. Use another sheet of paper, if necessary.

1. Some people may say that the anti-StinkCo people can start up their own newspaper. Is this a practical idea? Explain why or why not.

2. If the local newspaper refuses to print the anti-StinkCo advertisement, what other options are available to the people who oppose StinkCo? List and describe three.

   •

   •

   •

(continued)

Silence! -

3. Which of these three options do you think would be the most effective? Explain why.

Suppose that StinkCo has promised to enter into a contract with the local newspaper. The contract says that StinkCo will spend thousands of dollars on advertising in that newspaper each year. However, the contract requires that the newspaper refuse to publish any news stories that discuss the smell and smoke that come from the StinkCo factory.

4. If you were an executive at StinkCo, would you think this contract was a good idea or not? Explain your answer.

5. If you were the publisher of the newspaper, would you agree to sign the contract with StinkCo or not? Explain your answer.

Newsmakers- -

EACH FRIDAY EVENING, ABC's *World News Tonight* provides a story on its Person of the Week. This is someone who has done something very important in the world during the week.

Answer the following questions. Use another sheet of paper, if necessary.

1. Usually, the Person of the Week did something that most Americans consider good. Could the Person of the Week be somebody who did something that most Americans would consider bad? Explain why or why not.

2. Look through the newspapers of the past week. As you do so, identify the three people in the world that you consider a candidate for Person of the Week.

Person of the Week 1
Name:

Your reasons why she or he is one of the persons of the week:

Explain whether the person did something good or something bad:

Before you did this activity, had you heard of this person before?

Person of the Week 2
Name:

Your reasons why she or he is one of the persons of the week:

Explain whether the person did something good or something bad:

Before you did this activity, had you heard of this person before?

(continued)

Newsmakers -

Person of the Week 3

Name:

Your reasons why she or he is one of the persons of the week:

Explain whether the person did something good or something bad:

Before you did this activity, had you heard of this person before?

Each year in late December, *Time* magazine names its Person of the Year. Sometimes, the Person of the Year can be more than one person. For example, *Time*'s Person of the Year for 2003 was the American soldier.

4. Explain why you think *Time* named the American soldier the Person of the Year for 2003.

5. Do you think that *Time* made a good choice? Explain why or why not.

(continued)

Newsmakers -

6. Regardless of what time of the year that you are doing this activity, identify three people (or groups of people) that you believe are candidates for Person of the Year for the current year so far.

Person of the Year 1
Name:

   Your reasons why she or he is one of the persons of the year:

   Explain whether the person did something good or something bad:

Person of the Year 2
Name:

   Your reasons why she or he is one of the persons of the year:

   Explain whether the person did something good or something bad:

Person of the Year 3
Name:

   Your reasons why she or he is one of the persons of the year:

   Explain whether the person did something good or something bad:

Headlines -

ONE OF THE IMPORTANT responsibilities of a newspaper editor is to create an appropriate title, or headline, for each article that appears in a newspaper. Unlike many magazine articles, in which an article's writer may supply a title, newspaper editors often have to create their own title in the form of a headline for each article. This is because a headline must be relatively short—sometimes no more than three words—in order to get the reader's attention and to fit in a small space on the page. Sometimes, this is not easy to do!

Perform the following activity. Use another sheet of paper for your answers, if necessary.

1. Gather in groups of at least two people, as assigned by your teacher.

   • Without the other member(s) of the group watching, each member of the group should cut out six articles from a recent newspaper.

   • Identify each article by numbering them 1 to 6. Write the articles number twice, once next to each headline, and once at the end of the article.

   • After writing the same identifying number twice on each article, cut off the headline from each article (but save the headlines for later).

   • Give the six articles to another member of the group. Each member of the group will now have six numbered newspaper articles without headlines.

2. Read each article carefully and then create a good headline for each article. A good headline is one that quickly conveys the main point of each article. Each headline can be no more than four words long, with no more than twenty-four letters in each headline (spaces between words are not counted).

   Write each of your headlines below.

   Article 1 _____

   Article 2 _____

   Article 3 _____

   Article 4 _____

   Article 5 _____

   Article 6 _____

(continued)

Headlines- -

- After you have written the headlines, return the articles to the group member who gave them to you.

3. Now reread the six articles that have been returned to you, along with the suggested headlines that the other group member created. On a scale of 1 to 4, with 4 being the highest score and 1 the lowest score, grade each of the headlines created by your classmate. This grade should be based on how well each headline conveys the main point of each article. Give your scores below, and explain your reason for each. (Be fair! Remember that the other group member is also evaluating your work.)

	Low High	Reason for score
Article 1	1 2 3 4	
Article 2	1 2 3 4	
Article 3	1 2 3 4	
Article 4	1 2 3 4	
Article 5	1 2 3 4	
Article 6	1 2 3 4	

Now match the original headline for each article with the suggested headline from the other group member. Compare the two headlines and then explain which headline is better and why.

	Which headline is better? (newspaper's or group member's)	Why?
Article 1		
Article 2		
Article 3		
Article 4		
Article 5		
Article 6		

To Show or Not to Show? -

IN THE SPRING of 2004, many Americans and citizens of other countries were shocked and saddened to see photographs of American soldiers torturing Iraqi prisoners at the Abu Ghraib prison in Iraq. After seeing the pictures, President Bush condemned what he saw in the photographs, saying, "[I]t does not reflect the nature of the American people. That's not the way we do things in America. I didn't like it one bit." Several of the soldiers involved were punished for their involvement, and their commanding officers were disciplined. Although American television was the first news source to show the photographs of prisoner abuse, newspapers around the world reprinted the photographs.

Some Americans and others who opposed the United States' presence in Iraq used the photographs to support their criticism of the occupation. Some of the people who supported the occupation complained about the repeated showing of the photographs. For example, Col Allen, the editor-in-chief of the *New York Post,* said, "Clearly, the images are serving the political agenda of many newspapers." James Inhofe, a United States senator representing Oklahoma, said that he did not understand why some people were so upset about the photographs. Inhofe said, "I'm probably not the only one . . . that is more outraged by the outrage than we are by the treatment [of the prisoners] . . . Many of [the prisoners] probably have American blood on their hands and here we're so concerned about the treatment of those individuals."

Imagine that you are the editor of a daily newspaper. The United States is involved in a war against another nation that we will call Notmycountry. One of your reporters in the war zone photographs the abuse of Notmycountry prisoners of war by American troops.

Answer the following questions. Use another sheet of paper, if necessary.

1. What would be a good reason to publish the photographs? Explain your answer.

2. What would be a good reason not to publish the photographs? Explain your answer.

3. Would you publish the photographs? Explain why or why not.

(continued)

To Show or Not to Show? —

Once again, imagine that you are the editor of a daily newspaper. The United States is involved in a war against Notmycountry. One of your reporters photographs the abuse of Notmycountry citizens (not soldiers or prisoners of war) by American troops.

4. Explain how this situation is different from the situation involving photographs of torture of prisoners of war.

5. Would you publish the photographs of the American troops torturing Notmycountry citizens? Explain why or why not.

6. Explain why your answer to question 5 is different from or the same as your answer to question 3.

Another controversy regarding photography and the press arose during the U.S. military's involvement in Iraq in 2003–2004. Some newspapers and magazines published photographs of dead soldiers' flag-draped coffins arriving in the United States from Iraq. The military's official policy prohibits the photographing of soldiers' caskets. Military leaders say that these photographs violate the privacy of the dead soldiers and their families.

7. Do you agree that taking photographs of soldiers' caskets violates the privacy of the soldiers and their families? Explain why or why not.

Some of the people who have wanted photographs of soldiers' caskets published say that these photographs help remind us of the human costs of war.

8. Do you agree? Explain why or why not.

9. Imagine that you are a newspaper editor during the time of a military conflict. Would you publish photographs of dead soldiers' coffins? Explain why or why not.

Crime and Newspapers -

WHEN THE POLICE arrest somebody, that arrest is a matter of public record—if the arrestee is an adult, a newspaper can legally print his or her name. According to the American criminal justice system, a person is innocent until proved guilty. Many people who are arrested are not proved guilty at trial.

Answer the following questions. Use another sheet of paper, if necessary.

1. If you were the editor of a newspaper, would you print the names of all adults arrested in your community? Explain why or why not.

2. Would your answer to question 1 be different if one of your best friends or closest relatives were arrested? Explain why or why not.

As discussed in the Buzz in Unit 1, newspapers earn most of their money by selling advertising space. Imagine that you are the editor of a newspaper. One of your newspaper's largest advertisers is arrested for a serious crime.

3. What would be a good reason for publishing an article about this arrest?

4. What would be a good reason for not publishing an article about this arrest?

5. Would you publish an article about this arrest? Explain why or why not.

(continued)

Crime and Newspapers- -

Most states prohibit newspapers from printing the names of juveniles who are arrested.

6. Why do you think these states prohibit the printing of these names?

7. Do you think that the names of juveniles who are arrested should be printed in newspapers? Explain why or why not.

Criminal justice experts believe that rape is the most underreported serious crime in the United States. Because rape victims are often reluctant to complain, many states have enacted rape shield laws. These laws attempt to encourage rape victims to come forward. One common provision of rape shield laws is that newspapers cannot publish the alleged victim's name or photograph. However, the name of a person accused of rape can be published. Some observers complain that rape shield laws protect the alleged victim from newspaper publicity, but not the person accused of the crime. These observers say that this is unfair to the accused person, who is innocent until proved guilty.

8. Why do you think many rape victims do not want to complain to the police? Explain your answer.

9. Do you think that laws that prohibit newspapers from identifying alleged rape victims are a good idea? Explain why or why not.

The objectives of this unit are to help students

- recognize how gender, age, and race affect perception of oneself and of others
- distinguish magazine publishers' efforts to generate both culturally homogeneous and culturally diverse messages
- understand the impact that commercial interests have on magazines' content
- learn how to interpret and apply legislation to a variety of fact patterns

THE MAGAZINE PUBLISHERS of America web site (www.magazine.org) provides information that the association cites as "evidence about how magazines reach, connect, and influence teens *and* their purchase decisions" (emphasis added). Note the use of the conjunction; the association claims that magazines have influence on teenagers beyond matters of what to buy. Unlike daily newspapers, many magazines are directed specifically at teenagers. These magazines attempt to adopt the attitudes and worldviews of teenagers in order to appeal to them. Simultaneously, magazines also attempt to alter those attitudes and worldviews to suit the needs of magazines and their advertisers. This unit attempts to help students understand how magazines affect readers' attitudes about themselves and their relationships with others.

In this Unit . . .

Seventeen involves students in an assessment of the gender roles portrayed in this popular magazine.

Supermarket Tabloids has students examine the ethics of the publishers and the readers of these lurid and often cruel publications.

Paparazzi provides students with part of California's "anti-paparazzi" law. Students then determine whether the law would apply to different sets of circumstances.

The Colors and Sounds of Magazines has students investigate the future of magazines as the nation's ethnic diversity continues to increase.

Porno Mags asks students to evaluate the social costs and effects of pornography.

What Are the Issues in the Issues? has students explore and estimate the ways in which professional and trade publications react to social trends.

Money Changes Everything—or Does It? provides students with the opportunity to compare the social value and the economic value of people.

THE INTRODUCTION to this book mentioned that many teenagers do not read newspapers very often. Magazines are a different story, however. Few magazines seek a general readership today. Most magazine publishers and editors have identified a specific "niche" as their target market of readers. A *niche* is a small space. In the business world, "niche" refers to a specialized market of users, rather than everybody. For example, think about a product as popular as soft drinks. You might say to yourself, "Everybody drinks Coke or Pepsi." But when you visit the soft drink aisle in a grocery store, you can find Coke, Vanilla Coke, Cherry Coke, Coke C2, Diet Coke, Diet Caffeine-Free Coke, and so forth. Coca Cola also makes other soft drinks such as Sprite.

> **Magazines' primary purpose is to gather an audience for their advertisers.**

Similarly, while many people read magazines, they read different magazines based on a variety of factors. These factors include readers' age, gender, race and ethnicity, religious beliefs, interests, and hobbies. Other factors include where readers live, readers' education level, and how much money they have. As a result, there are thousands of different magazines published today.

Magazines aimed at teenagers view teen-agers as an "aspirational" market. Teenagers, as you are surely aware, are going through a dramatic amount of change in their lives. The teenage years are the time in life when many people begin to explore their life's ambitions, their sexuality, and their beliefs about how the world works. In many ways, teenagers are concerned about both where they are and where they are going in life. Magazine publishers and their advertisers know this. For example, General Motors places some of its advertisements for the Hummer in magazines that are read mostly by teenage males. The average teenage male can hardly afford a vehicle that costs more than $50,000. If he can afford a car at all, it is likely an older used car. However, the Hummer advertisements may help readers think that other General Motors cars are also desirable. If that older used car does not get very good gas mileage, hey—neither does a Hummer.

Advertisers and magazines geared toward teenagers are also aware that the teenage years are the time when people develop certain habits, including buying habits. For example, young women often develop preferences for brands of feminine hygiene products that they will continue to buy for many years. Teenage males often become loyal to particular brands of shaving products. Teenagers also develop loyalty for brands of products that are illegal for teenagers to use, such as beer and cigarettes.

Magazines' primary purpose is to gather an audience for their advertisers. Teenagers are attractive to advertisers. As a result, there are countless magazines directed toward teenage readers.

Seventeen -

ONE MAGAZINE widely read by teenage females in the United States is *Seventeen.* Most of the readers of *Seventeen* are actually younger than seventeen years old. (This is an example of an "aspirational" readership—many teenagers wish they were a few years older.) Although its readers are attracted to *Seventeen,* some people have criticized the magazine. They claim that although *Seventeen* often has information that is helpful to its readers, the magazine actually does more harm than good.

Look through a recent issue of *Seventeen,* and answer the following questions. Use another sheet of paper, if necessary.

1. Look at the females that appear in photographs in the magazine. Are most of the females that you know similar in weight? Explain why or why not.

A study of nine-year-old girls and teenage girls found an interesting result. Among the nine-year-old girls, 60 percent could say, "I feel happy the way I am." Among the teenage girls, only 29 percent could say this.

2. After looking through a copy of *Seventeen,* do you think the magazine helps its readers feel better about themselves, worse about themselves, or has no effect either way? Explain your answer.

According to the web site of Hearst Communications, the company that publishes the magazine, "*Seventeen* has been a significant force for change—creating notions of beauty and style, proclaiming what's hot in music and movies, identifying social issues, celebrating the idols and icons of popular culture."

3. Do you believe that a magazine is able to do these things? Or is this just hype? Or, is this partly true, partly hype? Explain your answer.

(continued)

Seventeen -

Imagine Marvin the Martian and Martina the Martian have traveled to Earth from Mars. They each pick up a copy of *Seventeen.* Neither of them knows anything about teenage earthlings other than what they see in the magazine. After looking through the pages of *Seventeen,* explain how you think Marvin and Martina would answer the following questions. Use another sheet of paper, if necessary.

4. According to *Seventeen,* what makes a teenage female happy? Explain your answer.

5. According to *Seventeen,* what do teenage males like the most about teenage females? Explain your answer.

6. According to *Seventeen,* do teenage females need a lot of money to be happy? Explain your answer.

7. According to *Seventeen,* what does it mean to be "feminine" on Earth? Explain your answer.

8. According to *Seventeen,* what does it mean to be "masculine" on Earth? Explain your answer.

9. Before Marvin and Martina return home to Mars, they ask you if their answers to questions 4 to 8 above are correct. Did *Seventeen* provide them with the correct information? Or is teenage reality different from the way the magazine portrays it? Explain your answer.

Supermarket Tabloids -

SUPERMARKET TABLOIDS are weekly magazines that feature stories on celebrities, strange occurrences, and fad diets. Most, although not all, of the articles about actors, musicians, and other famous people highlight their failings. Readers of supermarket tabloids often are presented with stories about celebrities' battles with weight or other health problems, drug and alcohol addiction, troubled romantic relationships, and professional difficulties.

Answer the following questions. Use another sheet of paper, if necessary.

1. Why do you think people like to read about the personal failings of celebrities? Explain your answer.

"Ethics" are a set of moral principles. To be "ethical" is to do what is morally correct under the circumstances.

2. Do you think that the publishers of supermarket tabloids are ethical? Explain why or why not.

3. Do you think that the readers of supermarket tabloids are ethical? Explain why or why not.

The United States Supreme Court has decided that there are different legal standards to be used when a publication prints something that is untrue about a famous person and when a publication prints something that is untrue about a person who is not famous. Because of this, it is harder for famous people to sue about untrue stories than it is for people who are not famous. The Court has basically said that celebrities who voluntarily place themselves in the public's eye are taking their chances with negative publicity.

(continued)

Supermarket Tabloids

4. Do you agree with the Supreme Court? Explain why or why not.

5. The actress Elizabeth Taylor once said, "There's no such thing as bad publicity." Explain what you think she meant by this.

One reason these publications are referred to as supermarket tabloids is that so many of them are sold in supermarkets. In fact, the great majority of these publications are sold by the single copy at retail stores rather than through mail subscriptions.

6. Why do you think that tabloids are usually bought one-at-a-time instead of by mail subscription?

Some of the best-known supermarket tabloids, including the *National Enquirer, Globe,* and *Star,* each lost more than ten percent of their circulation from 2002 to 2003.

7. Why do you think these tabloids lost readership? Explain your answer.

Paparazzi- -

YOU MAY ALREADY know that "paparazzi" is the common term for photographers who follow celebrities around. The word "paparazzi" comes from the name of a character in an old Italian movie. In 1999, California enacted the following law, which people call the "anti-paparazzi law."

> A person is liable for constructive invasion of privacy when the defendant attempts to capture, in a manner that is offensive to a reasonable person, any type of visual image, sound recording, or other physical impression of the plaintiff engaging in a personal or familial activity under circumstances in which the plaintiff had a reasonable expectation of privacy, through the use of a visual or auditory enhancing device, regardless of whether there is a physical trespass, if this image, sound recording, or other physical impression could not have been achieved without a trespass unless the visual or auditory enhancing device was used.
>
> California Civil Code 1708.8 (b)

Answer the following questions. Use another sheet of paper, if necessary.

1. This law was the first of its type in the United States. Why do you think California was the first state to pass such a law?

This law allows a person (the plaintiff) to sue another person (the defendant) for "constructive invasion of privacy." Another part of this law (not included here) talks about a "physical invasion of privacy."

2. What do you think the difference is between a constructive invasion of privacy and a physical invasion of privacy? Give an example of each type of invasion. (If you are not sure what "constructive" means, look it up in a dictionary.)

(continued)

Paparazzi- -

The law talks about "personal or familial activity" in which a person has a "reasonable expectation of privacy." Of course, any reasonable person would expect to have some privacy when using a bathroom.

3. List and describe three other situations where a person would have a reasonable expectation of privacy:

   -

   -

   -

When the law uses a "reasonable person" standard, the fact finder at trial decides how a reasonable person would react to something. If there is a jury, the jury acts as the fact finder. As you probably know, jurors are ordinary people from a community who are called for jury duty. (You will probably be called for jury duty someday.) The average juror is not a celebrity, and has not been followed around by paparazzi.

4. Do you think the average juror would be able to determine what a "reasonable" celebrity would find offensive? Explain why or why not.

5. Imagine that a photographer takes a picture of a famous movie star beating his wife. Do you think that the movie star should be able to sue the photographer under this California law successfully? Explain why or why not.

(continued)

Paparazzi –

Imagine that a photographer takes a picture of a celebrity and her family while the celebrity is celebrating her child's birthday in the family's backyard. For security reasons, the celebrity has tried to prevent the press from photographing her children. The photographer sells the picture to a magazine. The photographer does not work for the magazine. He took the photograph without first being told to by the magazine. The magazine publishes the photograph. The photographer is not rich, but the owners of the magazine are. Re-read the California law.

6. Will the celebrity be able to sue the owners of the magazine successfully? Explain why or why not.

7. The California law allows people to sue paparazzi for both actual and punitive damages. Explain what you think the difference is been actual damages and punitive damages, and give an example of each type of damage. (If you are not sure what "punitive" means, look it up in a dictionary.)

8. Do you think that California's anti-paparazzi law is a good law? Explain why or why not.

The Colors and Sounds of Magazines ------------------

ACCORDING TO THE United States Bureau of the Census, the nation's Hispanic and Asian populations will triple by 2050. The Bureau has predicted that the Hispanic population will increase 188 percent between 2000 and 2050. The Asian population will increase 213 percent. The African American population will increase by 71 percent. During this same period, the Bureau of the Census has predicted that the non-Hispanic white (sometimes called "Anglo" or "Caucasian") population will also increase, but only by about seven percent. Thus, by 2050, the Bureau believes that today's minority groups will together constitute a majority of the population. This change in the population will affect many aspects of American society.

Answer the following questions. Use another sheet of paper, if necessary.

1. Why do you think that Hispanic, African American, and Asian American groups are increasing at a much faster rate than the Anglo population? List and describe three reasons:

   -

   -

   -

Just because somebody calls himself or herself African American does not mean that this person has the same interests and beliefs as all other African Americans. In fact, some African Americans favor the term "black." Asian Americans come from many different heritages, religions, and languages. Some Hispanic people prefer to call themselves Latino. In addition, they may also describe themselves by race. Depending on the individual, a Hispanic or Latino person may describe their race as white, or as black, or as biracial.

2. Which do you think is more likely—that a Hispanic teenager likes the same types of music as an older Hispanic person? Or that a Hispanic teenager likes the same types of music as teenagers of other ethnic groups? Explain your answer.

(continued)

The Colors and Sounds of Magazines ----------------

3. Which do you think is more likely—that an Asian American teenager likes the same types of clothes as an older Asian American person? Or that an Asian American teenager likes the same types of clothes as teenagers of other ethnic groups? Explain your answer.

4. Which do you think is more likely—that an African American teenager likes the same types of magazines as an older African American person? Or that an African American teenager likes the same types of magazines as teenagers of other ethnic groups? Explain your answer.

5. Traditionally, some ethnic group members have liked spicy foods more than many Anglo people. However, more Americans, regardless of ethnicity, are enjoying spicy foods. Explain what you think has caused this shift in Americans' taste buds.

6. Although many hip-hop artists are African American, the majority of the people who listen to hip-hop music are Anglo. Explain why you think this is so.

The Buzz for this chapter discusses how magazines target different niches of readers. For example, *Ebony* magazine targets African American readers. There is no rule that says only African Americans can read this magazine. Nevertheless, most of *Ebony*'s readers are African American. Not all African Americans read *Ebony,* however. *Ebony*'s adult readership is 11.4 million, but there are more than 35 million African Americans in the United States.

7. Do you think that there will be more magazines directed at specific ethnic groups in the future? Fewer? Or about the same number as today? Explain your answer.

(continued)

The Colors and Sounds of Magazines - - - - - - - - - - - - - - - - -

You probably have heard American society referred to as a "melting pot." This expression is based on the belief that Americans of different cultures, races, religions, and languages have blended over the nation's history. Other people prefer to use the term "mosaic." This word comes from the belief that Americans have joined together while still maintaining individual cultural, racial, religious, and lingual (language) identities. There is no single correct answer as to whether the United States is a melting pot or a mosaic. The answer depends on how each of us wants to describe American society, as well as how we want to describe ourselves.

8. Is your racial or ethnic identity important to you? Explain why or why not.

As discussed throughout this book, most magazine publishers rely heavily on advertisers to make money.

9. Do you think that most *magazine publishers* want Americans to continue to identify themselves by their race or ethnicity in the future? Or do you think that *magazine publishers* would prefer Americans to think of themselves only as "American?" Explain your answer.

10. Do you think that most *advertisers* want Americans to continue to identify themselves by their race or ethnicity in the future? Or do you think that *advertisers* would prefer Americans to think of themselves only as "American?" Explain your answer.

Porno Mags -

THE FIRST AMENDMENT of the United States Constitution protects freedom of the press. This freedom extends to pornography. (*Pornography* is any material—including a magazine—that has explicitly sexual or erotic content.) However, the United States Supreme Court has said that the First Amendment does not protect all pornography. Some pornography may be classified as "obscene." This may happen when a jury finds that a particular pornographic item is clearly offensive to people in the community and that the item lacks serious literary, artistic, or scientific value. People who manufacture, distribute, and sell obscene items can be convicted of a crime. However, it is likely that the First Amendment protects all pornographic magazines that are sold at newsstands, bookstores, and convenience stores. It probably does not surprise you that these magazines are popular with many (but not all) young men.

The women and men who appear nude and perhaps engage in sexual conduct in pornographic magazines probably have some close friends and relatives.

Answer the following questions. Use another sheet of paper, if necessary.

1. If you just found out that a close relative or a close friend appeared in a pornographic magazine, how would you feel? Explain your answer.

2. Imagine that you are going to see the relative or friend who appeared in the pornographic magazine later today. What, if anything, would you say to that person about the photographs? Explain your answer.

Imagine that one of your best friends has just turned eighteen years old. She or he has been offered $1,000 to appear in a pornographic magazine. The photographic session will last less than four hours. Your friend asks you for your advice.

3. What are three good reasons that you could give your friend to try to discourage her or him from going to the photo session? List and describe each of them.

Reason 1:

Reason 2:

Reason 3:

(continued)

Porno Mags -

4. Do you think there are any good reasons to encourage your friend to pose for the photographs? Explain why or why not.

5. Would your answers to any of the four previous questions be different based on whether your friend or relative were male or female? Explain why or why not.

Imagine that you are twenty-four years old and have been dating the same person for almost a year. You discover that this person appeared nude in a pornographic magazine a few years before you started dating.

6. How would you feel? Explain your answer.

7. What, if anything, would you say to the person you have been dating? Explain your answer.

What Are the Issues in the Issues? -

YOU PROBABLY ALREADY know that there are many magazines devoted to body modifications such as piercing and tattooing. Most of these magazines celebrate body modifications and contain advertising for businesses that perform body modifications. You may not know that the cover story on the June 2004 issue of *RN,* a professional magazine directed toward nurses, discussed nursing care for patients with piercings.

This activity will not discuss body modifications. However, it will discuss how various professional and trade magazines deal with social trends. There are hundreds of magazines directed toward specific industries, professions, and businesses. For example, *Funeral Monitor* serves the mortuary industry, *Salon World* attracts readers in the beauty industry, and law enforcement officials subscribe to *Corrections Technology and Management.* Trade and professional magazines help people in an occupation stay current with important governmental and social events. These magazines often discuss new ideas and innovations. They also try to help people in the trade or profession to grow more profitable.

Answer the following questions. Use another sheet of paper, if necessary.

Beginning around 2003, the latest diet fad was the Atkins Diet. This diet emphasizes proteins such as meat and cheese and discourages eating many carbohydrates. Many types of bread and other bakery products are high in carbohydrates. So are many types of pasta and noodles.

There are trade magazines directed toward people in the Italian food and restaurant industry.

1. What types of articles do you think these magazines would publish in reaction to the popularity of the Atkins Diet? Explain your answer.

Several trade magazines are published for the airline industry.

2. What types of articles would you expect to find in these magazines after the events of September 11, 2001? Explain your answer.

Beginning around 2000, an increasing number of music fans chose to download their music from the Internet rather than buy it at stores. There are trade magazines directed to stores that sell recorded music on CDs.

(continued)

What Are the Issues in the Issues? - - - - - - - - - - - - - - - - - -

3. What types of articles would you expect to find in these magazines in reaction to music downloading? Explain your answer.

A survey of adult readers in 2004 found that fewer of them were reading literature than before. Bookstore owners subscribe to trade magazines aimed at their type of business.

4. What types of articles would you expect to find in these magazines in reaction to the fact that adults are reading less literature? Explain your answer.

Trade publications often discuss current government and legal issues that affect various industries. Think about some of the things that the government provides for its citizens, and then answer the following questions. (If you are not sure about your answer, discuss these questions with an older adult.)

5. Explain what types of government activities you think are discussed in trade magazines aimed at the cement and asphalt industries.

6. Explain what types of government activities you think are discussed in professional magazines directed toward doctors and other medical care providers.

7. Explain what types of government activities you think are discussed in trade magazines aimed at the automotive industry.

8. Explain what types of government activities you think are discussed in trade magazines aimed at industries that sell luxury goods, such as yachts, fur coats, and fine jewelry.

Money Changes Everything—or Does It? -------------

THE MAGAZINE PUBLISHERS OF AMERICA says that:

> Beyond the growth in the teen population, marketers cannot afford to ignore teens for numerous other reasons. This growing powerbase of spenders and influencers are important because they:
>
> • Have significant discretionary income
>
> • Spend family money as well as influence their parents' spending on both large and small household purchases
>
> • Establish and affect fashion, lifestyle, and overall trends
>
> • Provide a "window" into our society—a view of how it is now, and what it is likely to become

The last two bullets above are important to magazine publishers as they attempt to produce successful magazines in the future. Businesses, including magazine publishers, are constantly seeking "perfect information." Of course, there is no such thing as perfect information. If any of us had this information, we would always know which lottery numbers to choose, which line will be the fastest at the store, and what all the answers are on every test or quiz.

In this activity, we will focus on the first two points that the Magazine Publishers of America makes about teenagers. These first two points say that teenagers are important because of their buying power. You probably already know that the United States' economic system is founded on a capitalist, or market-based, economy. For example, petroleum companies, not the government, set gasoline prices. The petroleum companies charge whatever the "market will bear." In other words, they charge whatever consumers are willing to pay.

Answer the following questions. Use another sheet of paper, if necessary.

1. Most popular consumer magazines are priced between $2 and $6. Suppose the publisher of a magazine that was priced at $6 decided to charge $12 for the same magazine. Do you think the publisher would make twice as much money by doubling the price? Explain why or why not.

2. Imagine that the price of a magazine is $4. Does that magazine have the same value to every reader who buys the magazine for $4? Explain why or why not.

(continued)

Money Changes Everything—or Does It? - - - - - - - - - - - - -

Magazines provide readers with information about celebrities and other important people, such as political and business leaders. Many, although not all, of these people are considered rich.

3. Does the fact that a person is rich mean that he or she is an important person? Explain why or why not.

Many celebrities are rich because they can do things that ordinary people cannot do, such as write great songs, make exciting movies, or perform extraordinary athletic feats. Business and political leaders make decisions that affect the lives of many people.

4. Can a person become rich without providing anything of value to society? Explain why or why not.

Sociologists (experts who study how groups of people behave in society) have done secret studies of motorists' behavior in parking lots. One of the things they have found concerns those situations when two motorists want to park in the same parking space. Those sociologists discovered that people usually let somebody in a car that is nicer than their own have the space. People will usually not let somebody in a car that is not as nice as theirs have the parking space.

5. Explain what you think this information tells us about how people view money.

(continued)

Money Changes Everything—or Does It? - - - - - - - - - - - -

Not all of the people discussed in magazines are rich. For example, "ordinary" people who have had something very unusual happen to them are sometimes discussed in magazines (as when a woman who is not otherwise famous gives birth to quintuplets).

6. Look through some magazines. Find articles that discuss "ordinary" people. Identify three general reasons why these people are discussed in magazines. List and describe each of them below. One general reason is already given.

    Four General Reasons Why "Ordinary" People Are Discussed in Magazines

    • Something very unusual has happened to them.

    •

    •

    •

7. Imagine that the magazine *People* publishes an article about you someday because you are rich. What type of occupation or activity would you most like to be involved in that might make you rich? Explain your answer.

Not all rich people are famous. Many famous people are rich, but not all of them are.

8. If you could only be one or the other, which would you rather be: rich or famous? Explain your answer.

The objectives of this unit are to help students

- investigate and identify the boundaries of free speech
- balance the public's right to know with the individual's right to privacy
- express their imagination and creativity in writing
- develop their essay writing skills

THIS UNIT seeks to help students develop and articulate a variety of discussions about their relationships with newspapers and magazines. These discussions take the form of expressive writing, creative writing, expository writing, and a persuasive essay. The messages of newspapers and magazines are typically one-directional, from the publisher to the reader. This unit provides students with the chance to respond.

In this Unit . . .

The First Amendment and Teens has students evaluate the tension between the rights of student newspaper writers and the responsibilities of a school principal.

What Does What You Read Say About You? asks students to explore how magazine publishers and advertisers attempt to appeal to teenage readers. Students also identify how readers use the information in magazines in establishing and maintaining personal lifestyles.

Your Privacy Versus the Electronic Newspaper and Magazine has students investigate how the Internet helps publishers and advertisers gather personal data about readers.

Your Face in Print provides students with a series of dilemmas in which students weigh the rights of private individuals when their photographs are published.

Your Favorite Magazine has students write a five-paragraph persuasive essay arguing that their favorite magazine should be the favorite of other teenagers.

Rites of Passage asks students to examine the societal norms that underlie marriage, divorce, and adoption, and how these norms are reflected in newspapers' discussions of those events.

Your Obituary is intended to be a fun rather than morbid activity that provides students with the opportunity to use their imagination and creativity to compose an obituary and an epitaph for themselves.

THIS UNIT PLACES you in situations in which you have to make decisions about what we should or should not be able to say in newspapers and magazines. It also asks you to think about what newspapers and magazines should or should not be able to say about you.

The First Amendment of the United States Constitution protects freedom of the press, but the courts have never interpreted this as total freedom. We expect some friction in society. We will always be able to read things in newspapers and magazines that we do not agree with, that we think are stupid, or that many of us find offensive.

> **The First Amendment of the United States Constitution protects freedom of the press, but the courts have never interpreted this as total freedom.**

The First Amendment protects most of this information. However, the courts have to balance the interests of magazine and newspaper publishers and the interests of other people who claim that a newspaper or magazine has harmed them. This harm can include wrongfully damaging someone's reputation or invading someone's privacy.

However, most newspapers and magazines usually do not need to be concerned on a daily basis with First Amendment issues. They are more concerned with popular opinion. This is because newspapers and magazines must reflect society's interests in order to be profitable. If a newspaper or a magazine bores too many readers, it goes out of business. If a newspaper or a magazine offends too many readers, it goes out of business. If a newspaper or a magazine cannot attract readers who appeal to advertisers, it . . . well, you get the idea. Although newspapers and magazines are concerned with the laws and the courts, they are much more concerned with the marketplace.

Amendment I

Congress shall make no law respecting an establishment of religion, or prohibiting the free exercise thereof; or abridging the freedom of speech, or of the press; or the right of the people peaceably to assemble, and to petition the government for a redress of grievances.

The First Amendment and Teens -

YOU SHOULD BEGIN this activity by reviewing the wording of the First Amendment, which appears on the previous page. Do the students who write for your school newspaper enjoy First Amendment protection? In 1988, the United States Supreme Court decided that they do, but with some limitations. In the case of *Hazelwood* v. *Kuhlmeier,* students at a public high school in Missouri had written articles that their principal then deleted from the school newspaper. One article discussed teen pregnancies; the other discussed how their parents' divorcing affected teenagers. Although the court said that students do not "shed their constitutional rights to freedom of speech or expression at the schoolhouse gate," it also said that the rights of these students "are not automatically [the same as] the rights of adults in other settings." This is because, the court said, "[e]ducators are entitled to exercise greater control over . . . student expression to assure that participants learn whatever lessons the activity is designed to teach, that readers or listeners are not exposed to material that may be inappropriate for their level of maturity, and that the views of the individual speaker are not erroneously attributed to the school."

Answer the following questions. Use another sheet of paper, if necessary.

1. Do you agree with the court that students writing for a school newspaper should not have the same amount of freedom of the press that older adults have? Explain why or why not.

The court said that a school principal could delete a student newspaper article if that would "assure that [students] learn whatever lessons the activity is designed to teach."

2. What lesson would student newspaper writers and editors learn if their principal deleted one of their articles? Explain your answer.

(continued)

The First Amendment and Teens - - - - - - - - - - - - - - - - -

The court also said that a school principal could delete a student newspaper article so that "readers . . . are not exposed to material that may be inappropriate for their level of maturity."

   3. Do you think that an article about teen pregnancies is inappropriate for some high school students? Explain why or why not.

One of the principal's concerns about the article on teen pregnancies was that, even though the article did not give the names of the pregnant students, it would have been easy for readers to identify those students.

   4. Do you think the principal was correct when he deleted the article in order to protect the anonymity of the pregnant students? Explain why or why not.

Not all nine members of the United States Supreme Court agreed with this decision. Three judges joined in a dissenting opinion. They said that the school principal "violated the First Amendment's prohibitions against censorship of any student expression that neither disrupts classwork nor invades the rights of others."

   5. With whom do you agree—the six judges who said that a high school principal could delete the articles, or the three judges who said that the principal should not be able to delete the articles? Explain your answer.

(continued)

The First Amendment and Teens - - - - - - - - - - - - - - - - -

The Student Press Law Center warns high school students that the First Amendment does not protect students from being sued for invasion of privacy. The Center warns students that they "need to be aware that with press freedom does come legal responsibility."

Imagine that the principal in the *Hazelwood* case does not delete the article on teen pregnancies, and the article is published. Many students recognize the identity of one of the pregnant teens discussed in the article. She is very upset and sues for invasion of privacy.

It is safe to presume that the students who wrote the article have very little money of their own.

6. Should the pregnant student be able to sue the high school principal? Explain why or why not.

7. Should the pregnant student be able to sue the parents of the students who wrote the newspaper article? Explain why or why not.

The *Hazelwood* case involved a public high school. Government agencies operate public high schools. The government does not operate private high schools.

8. Do you think that students writing for a school newspaper at a private high school would have more rights of free press, fewer rights, or the same rights as student writers at a public school? Explain your answer.

What Does What You Read Say About You? ----------

EIGHTY PERCENT of teenagers read magazines on a regular basis. This translates into nearly 20 million magazine readers. A 2004 study also found that teenagers trust magazines more than other advertising media. Because most magazine publishers seek niches of readers rather than a broad readership, publishers work hard at making your favorite magazines feel like they belong to you. In this activity, we will evaluate whether magazine publishers are successful in this effort.

First, describe yourself. For each of the following questions, use three different adjectives to describe yourself. (If you are not sure what an adjective is, it is a word that describes a noun or pronoun, such as the word "green" in the phrase "the green car." In this case, the pronoun is *you*.)

1. Three adjectives that best describe you *as you actually are:*

2. Three adjectives that best describe you *as you would like to be:*

3. Three adjectives that best describe how you would like people your age to perceive you:

4. Three adjectives that best describe how you would like advertisers to perceive you:

5. Next, we will look at your interests. Describe the five activities you like doing the most when you are not in school:

   -
   -
   -
   -
   -

(continued)

What Does What You Read Say About You?---------

6. Now, we will look at your spending habits. List the top five things (products, services, or activities) on which you are *most likely* to spend your money:

   -
   -
   -
   -
   -

7. List the top five things (products, services, or activities) on which you would *most enjoy* spending your money (your answers here may be different from your answers to question 6):

   -
   -
   -
   -
   -

Before you answer the next questions, look through several magazines that you enjoy reading. This should especially include any magazines you subscribe to or buy on a regular basis. Use another sheet of paper for your answers, if necessary.

8. Do you believe that many of the other readers of these magazines are people like you? Explain why or why not, using specific examples of editorial articles or advertisements to support your answer.

(continued)

Activity 2 *(continued)*

What Does What You Read Say About You? - - - - - - - -

9. Do you believe that many of the other readers of these magazines are people with the same interests as you have? Again, explain why or why not, using specific examples of editorial articles or advertisements to support your answer.

10. Review your answers to questions 6 and 7. Are many of the advertisements in these magazines for the types of products, services, or activities that you listed in those questions? Explain why or why not.

Jane Rinzler Buckingham, the president of Youth Intelligence, a marketing firm that focuses on teenagers and other young people, said, "[Teenagers] will go to magazines that become life-stylists for them. Because what they're hoping to get is some sort of vision of how they can be the best that they can be. In terms of some of what we're hearing about magazines, magazines are the filters to their world."[3]

11. Is what Buckingham says true about most teenagers? Explain why or why not.

12. Is what Buckingham says true about you? Explain why or why not.

---

[3]http://www.magazine.org/content/files/teenprofile04.pdf

Your Privacy Versus the Electronic Newspaper and Magazine ------------------

YOU PROBABLY ALREADY know that it is almost impossible to be anonymous when we use the Internet. Although some publishers fear the shift from printed newspapers and magazines to electronic versions, many are very excited. Perhaps the most significant feature of the Internet for publishers and advertisers is that it allows interactivity. This means that instead of a publication and its advertisements being a "one-way street" with the information coming only from the publisher and advertisers, the Internet allows advertisers to receive communications from consumers.

This is not because publishers and advertisers like you and think you're cool! Each time you visit a web site and click on a link to an article or click on a banner advertisement, you provide feedback to publishers and advertisers. This allows publishers to find out quickly what types of articles are interesting to readers and which ones are not. Publishers use this information to gather a larger audience for their advertisers. Interactivity allows advertisers to find out which advertising messages work and which ones do not work.

Interactivity also allows publishers and advertisers to build a database about consumers, which helps advertisers to conduct **data mining.** For example, if a teenager subscribes to a magazine, the magazine and its advertisers may know nothing about that subscriber except his or her name and address. Inside the magazine, a contest or an opinion poll might be featured that asks the reader to go to the magazine's web site. Once there, the magazine can ask for demographic and psychographic information about the reader: his or her age, hobbies, likes and dislikes, and so forth. Or an advertisement inside the magazine might contain the advertiser's web site address and encourage readers to go to that site. The advertiser's web site might ask for similar demographic and psychographic information.

Answer the following questions. Use another sheet of paper, if necessary.

1. Publishers and advertisers have found that teenagers are the age group most likely to participate in contests, opinion polls, and other activities that require readers to provide information about themselves. Why do you think teenagers are more likely to participate than older adults are? Explain your answer.

(continued)

Your Privacy Versus the
Electronic Newspaper and Magazine -------------

2. One of the challenges for publishers and advertisers when they try to find out about teenagers' likes and dislikes is that teenagers are a "moving target." What do you think they mean by the term "moving target"? Explain your answer.

Go to the web site of a magazine that is popular with you and your friends. Look around the site, and count how many ways this site tries to gather information about you.

3. Describe what you found.

4. How do you think the magazine and its advertisers will use this information?

A survey conducted in 2000 found that one in three Internet users between the ages of seven and sixteen were willing to give out their home address over the Internet in order to receive free samples, gifts, or information. The Children's Online Privacy Protection Act (COPPA) does not allow the collection of any personal information from anyone under the age of thirteen without parental consent. This is just one of the reasons why web sites ask about your birth date.

5. Do you think the average thirteen-year-old is worried about privacy risks on the Internet? Explain your answer.

(continued)

Your Privacy Versus the
Electronic Newspaper and Magazine – – – – – – – – – – – – – –

6. *Should* a thirteen-year-old worry about privacy risks on the Internet? Explain why or why not.

Imagine that a teen-oriented magazine asks its readers to identify their favorite movie stars and musicians.

7. How long do you think the information from this poll will be current? Explain your answer.

8. Why do you think teenagers' preferences for movie stars and musicians change?

9. Which age group do you think changes its preferences for movie stars and musicians more often—teenagers or adults in their forties? Explain your answer.

Your Face in Print -

YOU MAY HAVE HEARD about certain groups of people who do not want their photograph taken. Some of these people say that taking their picture amounts to taking their soul. Most people do not have this interpretation of photography. However, there are situations when we do not want our photograph taken; there are certainly situations in which we do not want our photograph published in a magazine.

Answer the following questions. Use another sheet of paper, if necessary.

Imagine that you are injured in a serious car accident on a highway. (We hope this never happens!) A photograph of you, bleeding and obviously in pain, is published in a local newspaper without your permission. The photograph appears above a news article about the accident.

1. Do you think that you should be able to sue the newspaper for having published your photograph without your permission?

The following question presumes some of the same circumstances as question 1. You are injured in a serious car accident on a highway. A photograph of you bleeding and obviously in pain is published. However, the photograph does not appear in a newspaper, as in question 1. In this situation, the photograph appears in a trade magazine directed toward people in the cement industry. The article in which your photograph appears discusses why the cement industry needs to try to get more money from the government to build safer highways.

2. Many people would argue that you would have a better chance to sue successfully in this situation than in the situation presented in question 1. Explain why.

(continued)

Your Face in Print- -

One day you have the opportunity to meet one of your favorite celebrities, Bigg Schott. He signs an autograph for you and agrees to have his picture taken with you. A friend takes a photograph of you and the celebrity. A professional photographer who is following the celebrity around also takes a photograph of the two of you.

The professional photographer's photograph of you and Schott appears in a local newspaper. The photograph appears with a news story about Schott's visit to your community.

3. Do you think that you should be able to sue the newspaper for publishing the photograph without your permission? Explain why or why not.

Unfortunately, the week after the photograph was taken, Schott is arrested for a serious crime. A news magazine publishes the photograph of you and the celebrity together. The magazine does not publish your name, only that of Schott.

4. Do you think that you should be able to sue the magazine for publishing the photograph without your permission? Explain why or why not.

Presume some of the same circumstances as in question 4, except that the magazine *does* publish your name below the photograph of you and Schott.

5. Do you think this gives you a better chance to sue successfully than it did in the situation in question 4? Explain why or why not.

(continued)

Your Face in Print -

Again, presume some of the same circumstances as in question 4, except that the magazine publishes the **caption,** "Famous celebrity and accused criminal Bigg Schott meets with one of his loyal fans."

The magazine article does not mention that your photograph with Schott was taken *before* he was arrested.

6. Some lawyers would say that the caption places you in a "false light." Explain what you think they mean by this.

We will now switch to a new set of circumstances. Imagine that you heroically save someone from a car that has been driven into a pond. A newspaper photographer arrives on the scene while you are bravely helping the motorist. Your photograph appears in the next day's newspaper. However, the caption below the photograph misidentifies the two of you. The caption identifies you as the victim and the victim as the hero. You call the newspaper and ask the editor to publish a correction. The editor refuses to do so.

7. What would you do next? Explain your answer.

Your Favorite Magazine -

ACCORDING TO the Magazine Publishers of America, the favorite magazines of teenage females and teenage males in 2003 were:

Teenage Females

1. *YM*
2. *Seventeen*
3. *Teen People*
4. *Allure*
5. *Vibe*
6. (tie) *In Style*
6. (tie) *Glamour*
7. *Marie Claire*
8. (tie) *Vogue*
8. (tie) *Source*
9. *Self*
10. *Cosmopolitan*

Teenage Males

1. *Dirt Rider*
2. *Four Wheeler*
3. *WWE Magazine*
4. *4 Wheel & Off Road*
5. *Motorcyclist*
6. *Sport Truck*
7. *Popular Hot Rodding*
8. *Car Craft*
9. (tie) *Street Rodder*
9. (tie) *Truckin'*
10. *Cycle World*

You may or may not see your favorite magazine listed here. You probably noticed that the popular magazines among teenage females are mostly fashion magazines, and the popular magazines among teenage males are mostly car and motorcycle magazines.

Answer the following questions. Use another sheet of paper, if necessary.

1. Explain why you think many teenage females are interested in fashion magazines.

2. Do you think this interest changes as females grow older? Explain why or why not.

3. Explain why you think many teenage males are interested in car and motorcycle magazines.

(continued)

Activity 5 *(continued)*

Your Favorite Magazine -

4. Do you think this interest changes as males grow older? Explain why or why not.

Imagine the publisher of your favorite magazine has asked you to recruit more readers. The publisher wants to use the words of its readers to tell other teens why the magazine is their favorite. The publisher asks you to write a five-paragraph persuasive essay. This essay will emphasize three good reasons to read the magazine. Tips on how to write a five-paragraph persuasive essay are in the box below.

5. Using these tips, write a five-paragraph essay that will persuade others to read your favorite magazine.

The Five-Paragraph Persuasive Essay

I. Introductory Paragraph with Thesis Statement

The thesis is the argument that you are trying to persuade the reader to agree with. In this case, your thesis is simple: you are going to tell the reader that your favorite magazine should be his or her favorite, too. In the introductory paragraph, you will also list the three pieces of evidence that you will use in the body of the essay. In this case, your evidence is your three reasons why other people should read your favorite magazine.

II. Body: First Piece of Evidence

It is best to analyze your three pieces of evidence and evaluate how strong each argument is, then rank them 1, 2, 3. Because you want to have a strong finish, many people recommend saving the strongest argument for last. However, because you do not want to get off to a bad start, begin the body of the essay with your second-strongest argument. In this way, you can "hide" your weakest argument in the middle. Make certain that you have a transition between each argument. Each of the paragraphs of the body should lead into the next paragraph.

III. Body: Second Piece of Evidence

Present your weakest argument.

IV. Body: Third Piece of Evidence

Present your strongest argument.

V. Conclusion

Restate your thesis, and include the three points you have used to prove that thesis.

Rites of Passage

THE TERM "rites of passage" applies to those events that mark significant changes in our lives. The first rite of passage is, of course, birth. Newspapers announce the births of children born locally. Both newspapers and magazines often publish information about the births of children born to celebrities. Another common rite of passage is marriage. Again, newspapers typically announce the marriages of local couples. Both newspapers and magazines may announce the marriages of celebrities. If marriages end in divorce, this information is also published. (Activity 7 discusses death announcements.)

In the past few years, many daily newspapers have changed the title of their wedding announcements section. Over 140 newspapers, including the *Boston Globe* and the *Los Angeles Times,* now call their former "Marriages and Engagements" section the "Special Occasions" or "Celebrations" section.

Answer the following questions. Use another sheet of paper, if necessary.

1. Explain why you think that these newspapers have changed the name of this part of the newspaper.

2. Do you think that it was a good idea to change the name of this section? Explain why or why not.

3. Would you like to get married someday? Explain why or why not.

4. If you got married, would you want information about your marriage published in a local newspaper? Explain why or why not.

(continued)

Rites of Passage -

If a couple has a legally valid marriage, they must go to a state court to get a divorce. Because the government grants divorces, information about divorces is a matter of public record. When information is a matter of public record, newspapers and magazines may legally publish this information, although they are not required to. As you know, some people are embarrassed about getting divorced.

5. Imagine that you are the editor of a national magazine. Would you publish information about the divorce of a famous celebrity? Explain why or why not.

6. Imagine that you are the editor of a local newspaper. Would you publish information about the divorce of two ordinary local people who are not famous? Explain why or why not.

7. Review your answers to questions 5 and 6. Explain why your answers to those two questions are either different or the same.

8. Imagine that you are married and the marriage is unfortunately ending in divorce. Explain how you would feel if information about your divorce were published in a local newspaper.

(continued)

Rites of Passage ----------------------------------

As you know, many children are adopted by people who are not their birth parents. Because a state government must authorize an adoption, some information about an adoption is a matter of public record.

9. Explain why some people do not want information about adoptions published.

10. Do you agree with those people? Explain why or why not.

11. Imagine that you have decided to adopt a young child. Would you want information about that adoption published? Explain why or why not.

Your Obituary -

ACCORDING TO the United States Center for Disease Control, an American female born in the 1990s could expect to live for about seventy-nine years. American males born during the same period could expect to live for about seventy-three years. Of course, these are averages. Some people suffer from a fatal illness while relatively young. Others die in accidents and homicides.

Answer the following questions. Use another sheet of paper, if necessary.

1. Why do you think the average life expectancy for females is longer than for males? Explain your answer.

Life expectancies for Americans changed dramatically in the twentieth century. For example, an American female born in 1900 had an average life expectancy of forty-eight years. For males born that year, the average life expectancy was forty-six years. Improvements in medical care have contributed to the increase in life expectancy.

2. List two other factors that you believe have increased people's life expectancy. Explain your answers.

- Reason 1 for Increased Life Expectancy:

  Explanation:

- Reason 2 for Increased Life Expectancy:

  Explanation:

When people die, their passing is often noted in newspapers. Sometimes, there is simply a death notice. This tells readers when the person died, and whether there will be a funeral or other celebration of that person's life. At other times, a person's death will be noted by an obituary. An obituary provides some biographical information about the person who has died. The obituary may tell us about the dead person's childhood and education, his or her family, his or her professional life, and other information about that person that readers may find interesting. If the person is noteworthy or famous, hundreds of newspapers throughout the United States and the rest of the world may publish an obituary. To get some idea about what obituaries contain, read some of them in a local newspaper before completing the next part of this activity.

(continued)

Your Obituary -

3. Assume that you have lived the kind of life you hope to live. You may die in your sleep at the ripe old age of 100. You may die much earlier in life while heroically saving people during a natural disaster. For the purposes of this activity, that is all up to you. Write your obituary. Use another sheet of paper.

   • Use your imagination!

   • Be certain to tell readers basic information about your childhood and education. (Did you go to a prestigious Ivy League college? Or did you run away and join the circus?)

   • Include information about your family life. (Did you have twelve kids? Were you childless? Was anybody in your family famous or noteworthy?)

   • Also discuss your career. (Were you a scientist? Were you a hip-hop star? Were you both?)

   • Add any other information you want to about your hobbies, interests, and so forth.

We call the words on a person's tombstone an epitaph. Epitaphs tend to be short—rarely longer than a dozen or so words. Most epitaphs are solemn and serious. However, some epitaphs can be quite funny. For example, there is supposedly a tombstone in Albany, New York, with the epitaph for a man named Harry Edsel Smith. Smith's epitaph reads:

> Born 1903–Died 1942
> Looked up the elevator shaft to see if
> the car was on the way down. It was.

4. Write your tombstone's epitaph. It can be as serious or as humorous as you want it to be. Again, use your imagination!

The objectives of this unit are to help students

- develop their knowledge of financial and economic issues
- recognize how advertisers' agendas influence publishers' editorial decisions
- evaluate the need for government regulation of publishers' business practices
- identify ethical considerations in publishing and in their own lives

IT IS DIFFICULT for a reader to miss the commercial aspect of newspapers and magazines. However, many readers, including teenagers, are unaware that advertisers' influence extends well beyond the discrete advertisements that appear on the page. This unit provides students with a set of activities that help them recognize that publishers' economic agenda extends into the editorial copy of newspapers and magazines. Students also explore how others outside the publishing industry use newspapers and magazines to achieve financial gain. The activities use examples of both macroeconomic and microeconomic principles to facilitate student learning.

In this Unit . . .

Circulation asks students to assess the future of magazine readership. Students also identify some of the issues that publishers consider when setting magazine prices.

Complementary Copy has students evaluate the ethics of the editorial practice of placing articles in magazines that benefit advertisers.

It's All About the Advertising asks students to calculate what percentage of a magazine of their choosing is advertising. They also investigate the methods advertisers use to get readers' attention.

The Big Guy Versus the Little Guy provides students with information about economies of scale. Students use this information to explore the effect that this economic principle has on magazine advertising.

Newspapers, Magazines, and Synergy has students examine the impact that cross-ownership of media has on the information presented in print media.

The Want Ads asks students to evaluate how newspapers' employment advertisements reflect societal norms.

The Ethics of the "Advertorial" engages students in an examination of the ethics of the common publishing practice of confusing advertising material and editorial material. This activity also includes a suggested group activity in which students create codes of ethics for students at their school.

THE PRICE YOU PAY for a newpaper or magazine subscription or for a single copy of a newspaper or magazine usually represents only a very small part of the income that the publication receives. Most newspapers and magazines are primarily advertising delivery vehicles. Yes, that sounds fancy. The point is that most newspapers and magazines make much more money for their owners through the selling of advertisements in those publications than they do through circulation.

> **Most newspapers and magazines are primarily advertising delivery vehicles.**

Almost all newspapers are directed toward particular communities. Thus, although newspapers often have advertisements for products available nationally, most newspaper advertisements are for local businesses. In many communities, department stores are heavy newspaper advertisers. There are only a few newspapers that serve a national audience. These include the *Wall Street Journal* and *USA Today*.

Most magazines are aimed at a national readership. Although there are regional and local magazines (*Texas Monthly* and *Boston* are examples), most magazine advertisers are usually not concerned about where a magazine's readers live. Rather, magazine advertisers are concerned with what readers' interests are. For example, there are probably hundreds of music magazines. Some music magazines are designed to appeal to people who like hip-hop, others try to appeal to jazz fans, and so forth. Many music magazines are aimed at musicians. Which magazine a musician reads may depend on which type of instrument or which type of music he or she plays.

There are thousands of magazines circulating in the United States today. Advertisers choose which magazines to advertise in based on several factors, including circulation, the demographics of readers, and the psychographics of readers. For example, both *Sports Illustrated* and *ESPN the Magazine* are aimed at sports fans. *Sports Illustrated* sells more than 3.2 million copies a month. *ESPN the Magazine* sells about half that many copies. However, *ESPN the Magazine* is oriented toward younger readers. Thus, a company that makes products aimed at teenagers may be more likely to advertise in *ESPN the Magazine*, although *Sports Illustrated* has more readers overall.

Newspapers are also concerned about demographics and psychographics. One demographic aspect that is attractive to advertisers is the fact that people who read newspapers tend to be better educated and make more money than people who do not read newspapers regularly. If a community has two or more competing newspapers, the editors of each paper will probably attempt to attract certain psychographic groups. For example, one newspaper may target people who tend to vote for Democrats, while another paper will target people who usually vote for Republicans. However, today only a few large communities still have more than one daily newspaper.

Circulation---

THE PEOPLE WHO SELL advertising space in magazines and newspapers like to emphasize their publication's readership, or audience, rather than its circulation. A single copy of a magazine mailed to one's home has a paid circulation of one, but may have a readership of five. This is because five people in the home may read that magazine. A copy of a magazine going to an office or a library will likely have an even higher readership.

Answer the following questions. Use another sheet of paper, if necessary.

1. After peaking in 2000, total magazine circulation in the United States has been decreasing each year for the past few years. List and describe three reasons why you think this has happened.

   Reason 1:

   Reason 2:

   Reason 3:

2. Do you think that total magazine circulation will continue to decrease in the future, or do you think that this trend will change? Explain your answer.

Imagine that you are the publisher of a weekly local magazine that is aimed at teenagers. This magazine features articles that teenagers are interested in, including music, movies, and fashion. Many local businesses advertise in your magazine, and most of your income comes from advertising, not circulation. You are currently charging $1 for each issue of your magazine. However, the owner of the magazine has asked you whether it is a good idea to distribute the magazine for free.

(continued)

Circulation- -

3. From the magazine owner's point of view, what is a good reason for distributing the magazine for free? Explain your answer.

4. From the magazine owner's point of view, what is a good reason to continue charging $1 for each issue? Explain your answer.

5. Before deciding whether to stop charging for the magazine, what additional information would you need? Explain your answer.

6. Why might some advertisers be doubtful about advertising in a magazine that is distributed for free? Explain your answer.

7. What would you tell those doubtful advertisers that would encourage them to advertise in your magazine if it were distributed for free? Explain your answer.

Complementary Copy -

THE PEOPLE WHO WORK in the publishing industry use the term "copy" to refer to the words that make up articles and stories. Advertisers often expect magazines to provide "complementary copy" for their advertisements. This means advertisers want a magazine's editors to place articles in the magazine that will help the advertiser sell more of its product. For example, a company that makes margarine will choose to advertise in food magazines that include recipes using margarine. The editors of food magazines will often try to place some of these recipes on the page opposite from a margarine advertisement.

Answer the following questions. Use another sheet of paper, if necessary.

1. If the government released a study saying a certain type of food was bad for one's health, do you think a food magazine that often includes several advertisements for that type of food would report this study to its readers? Explain why or why not.

2. Look through several magazines and find three examples of complementary copy. If possible, cut out each advertisement and the copy that complements it. Explain why each is an example of complementary copy.

Example 1
   Product being advertised:
   Description of complementary copy:

Example 2
   Product being advertised:
   Description of complementary copy:

Example 3
   Product being advertised:
   Description of complementary copy:

(continued)

Complementary Copy -

3. Using the following five-point scales, evaluate the practice of magazines providing complementary copy for their advertisers. Circle the number that best represents your opinion.

Dishonest   1   2   3   4   5   Honest

Explain the reason for your rating:

Unfair to readers   1   2   3   4   5   Fair to readers

Explain the reason for your rating:

Bad way to make money   1   2   3   4   5   Good way to make money

Explain the reason for your rating:

4. If you were a magazine editor, would you place complementary copy in the magazine for your advertisers? Explain why or why not.

It's All About the Advertising -

THE FINANCIAL SUCCESS of almost all magazines and newspapers depends on advertising. In many magazines there are more—often many more—pages of advertising than there are of editorial material. According to *Guinness World Records,* the most advertising pages in a single magazine occurred in the February/March 2001 American edition of *Bride's,* which contained 1,090.75 pages of advertisements (out of a total of 1,286 pages).

Answer the following questions. Use another sheet of paper, if necessary.

Look through a magazine that you find interesting.

1. First, count the total number of pages in the magazine, and write the answer below.

2. Then, count the number of pages of advertisements. For advertisements that occupy less than an entire page, use fractions in decimal form. For example, a half-page advertisement would count as .5, a quarter-page advertisement would count as .25, and so on. Write the answer below.

3. Divide your answer for question 2 by your answer for question 1. Write that answer below.

   This is the percentage of your magazine that is devoted to advertising. (For example, if the answer to question 2 is 128, and the answer to question 1 is 200, 128 divided by 200 is equal to .64 or 64 percent.)

4. Were you surprised at the answer to question 3? Explain why or why not.

(continued)

It's All About the Advertising -

5. Because magazines have so many pages of advertisements, advertisers have to fight through the clutter. Look through a magazine, searching for three different ways advertisements try to get your attention. Describe each of them below.

   First method of attracting your attention:

   Second method of attracting your attention:

   Third method of attracting your attention:

The location of an advertisement often determines its price. People in the publishing business call the right hand page the "recto" and the left hand page the "verso."

6. Which do you think costs more—the right-hand (odd-numbered) page or the left-hand (even-numbered) page? Explain why.

7. Which do you think costs more—an advertisement inside the front cover of a magazine or an advertisement inside the back cover of a magazine? Explain why.

(continued)

It's All About the Advertising -

Because of the way our eyes move as we skim through a magazine, advertising agencies often design the layout of their advertisements to follow the general shape of the letter Z, as shown below.

Look through a magazine and find an advertisement that follows this rule. (You will not find an actual letter Z, but you should be able to find an advertisement that is arranged to follow the shape of the letter.)

8. Explain why you think the advertisement you selected follows the letter-Z rule.

9. Why do you think our eyes usually move in the form of the letter Z when we skim through a magazine? Explain your answer.

10. Who pays for magazine and newspaper advertising—the advertiser or the person who buys the advertised product? Explain your answer.

The Big Guy Versus the Little Guy -

BEFORE THE AGE of heavily advertised branded products, local merchants could sell whatever they wanted to and price their goods at whatever people were willing to pay for them. Most importantly, the general store's merchandise goods were unbranded. For example, a customer would simply ask the merchant for a quart of cooking oil, rather than ask for Crisco, Wesson, or some other brand of oil. The merchant would store the oil in unbranded barrels, and pump out whatever the customer needed into a plain, unmarked jar.

As discussed in Unit 1, the magazine industry experienced a boom beginning in the middle of the nineteenth century. Many magazines were (and still are) sold at newsstands. However, many magazine publishers also relied heavily on subscribers who received their magazines in the mail (and still do). In 1863, the United States Post Office (predecessor to today's United States Postal Service) established three classes of mail and allowed magazines to be mailed at the second-class rate. You probably already know that the cost of sending mail depends on weight. The more an item weighs, the more it costs to mail that item.

Many local merchants complained when the Post Office allowed magazine publishers to use a second-class rate rather than the more expensive first-class rate used for letters. This is because the general store owner found it difficult to compete against mass manufacturers. As magazines with advertisements for mass-manufactured goods became more common, readers began asking for specific brands of goods when they shopped at their local stores. These branded items cost the local merchant more than unbranded items did.

The local merchant also lost business when readers used mail order to buy goods directly from the manufacturer rather than from the local merchant. Advertisements in magazines allowed manufacturers to promote their mail order services. Lowering the price of mailing a magazine made it less expensive, and thus easier, for manufacturers of branded products to hurt general stores even more.

Imagine that you are the owner of a general store in 1880. Previously, you had been selling unbranded (but high quality) products to your customers. However, because of magazine advertising, more and more of your customers are asking for specific brands of products by name.

(continued)

The Big Guy Versus the Little Guy — — — — — — — — — — — — — — — —

Answer the following questions. Use another sheet of paper, if necessary.

1. If you politely refused to sell those branded products, what do you think would happen? Explain your answer.

2. If you decided to replace your unbranded products with the branded products that customers asked for, what do you think would happen to your profits? Explain your answer.

Economists talk about *economies of scale*. This means that it usually costs less per unit to make one million items than it does to make ten items. We will use just one of many manufacturing costs to explain. Imagine that it costs a manufacturer $1,000,000 to build a factory. If it makes only ten items in that building, the factory overhead expense for each item is $100,000 ($1,000,000 divided by 10 equals $100,000). If one million items are made in that building, the factory expense for each item is $1 ($1,000,000 divided by 1,000,000 equals $1).

Similarly, it usually costs less per unit to sell one million items than it does to sell ten items. This is one reason that the price of merchandise at Wal-Mart (the largest retailer in the world) is often lower than it is at a small, locally owned store. Because Wal-Mart has better economies of scale, it can sell its goods at lower prices. Since Wal-Mart's low prices allow people to buy more, its economies of scale continue to grow even larger.

3. Explain how magazine advertising leads to economies of scale for the companies that advertise in magazines.

(continued)

The Big Guy Versus the Little Guy -

4. Explain how economies of scale influenced the Post Office when it decided to allow magazines to be mailed at a less expensive rate.

5. Some people complain that allowing magazine publishers to send mail at a lower rate than consumers generally pay results in consumers subsidizing those publishers. *Subsidizing* means that consumers who pay the first-class rate for mail are helping to pay for the discount that the Postal Service gives to publishers that use the lower second-class rate. The Postal Service responds that this is not true. It says that it is simply passing the benefit of economies of scale through to publishers who may mail millions of magazines each year. Whom do you agree with—the people who complain about subsidization, or the Postal Service? Explain your answer.

6. You probably already know that heavily advertised products are usually more expensive than similar, unadvertised, "no name" products. If advertising helps improve economies of scale, why do products that are heavily advertised in magazines usually cost more? Explain your answer.

7. Imagine that you want to start up a new company that makes perfumes and colognes. Do you think your company can be successful if you do not advertise your products in magazines? Explain why or why not.

Newspapers, Magazines, and Synergy - - - - - - - - - - - - - - -

SYNERGY is the coordinated interaction between two or more organizations, designed to create a combined effect that is greater than the results those organizations could have each had on their own. For example, if *ESPN the Magazine* encourages its readers to watch ESPN on television, and ESPN television encourages its viewers to read *ESPN the Magazine,* the magazine is helping the television network to make more money, and vice versa. The Walt Disney Company owns both *ESPN the Magazine* and ESPN the television network, creating yet another type of synergy, especially during the years when Disney owned both the Mighty Ducks of Anaheim hockey team and the Anaheim Angels baseball team.

(To understand better how media companies try to create synergies, you may want to check out the *Columbia Journalism Review's* "Who Owns What" web site: www.cjr.org/tools/owners.)

Answer the following questions. Use another sheet of paper, if necessary.

1. What synergies could result if a magazine publisher bought a paper mill? Explain your answer.

2. What synergies could result If a magazine publisher bought a newspaper? Explain your answer.

3. What synergies could result if a magazine publisher bought a television station? Explain your answer.

(continued)

Newspapers, Magazines, and Synergy - - - - - - - - - - - - -

4. Suppose you read a magazine that reviews a new music CD. If the music company that released the CD was owned by the same company that publishes the magazine, do you think that the music review could be biased? Explain why or why not.

5. Suppose you read a story in your local newspaper about a television actor. The television actor stars on a program broadcast by a television station owned by the newspaper's publisher. What kinds of things do you think that the newspaper would write about that actor? Explain your answer.

6. Companies that own newspapers and magazines also own some of the companies that publish school textbooks. Do you think this fact has any impact on the things that are written in your textbooks and taught in your school? Explain why or why not.

7. Do synergies in the media industry provide benefits to consumers? Or do synergies in the media industry hurt consumers? Or both? Explain your answer.

The Want Ads -

IF YOU HAVE NOT done so yet, it is likely that some time in the next few years you will use a newspaper to search for a job. The employment section of newspapers, also known as the "help wanted" section or simply the "want ads," appears in the classified section of most daily newspapers each day or each week in weekly newspapers.

Answer the following questions. Use another sheet of paper, if necessary.

1. Many people say that the best job openings do not appear in the newspaper. Explain why you think they say this. (If you are not sure, ask an older adult about this.)

2. Do you agree? Explain why or why not.

3. Do you think this is fair to people? Explain why or why not.

4. In most daily newspapers, the largest collection of employment advertisements appears in the Sunday edition. Explain why you think this is the case.

5. Explore the Sunday employment advertisements from a local newspaper. Identify at least three types of jobs that would not have been included in the employment advertisements 100 years ago. List each job and explain why that job was not available 100 years ago.

   •

   •

   •

(continued)

The Want Ads -

6. Identify at least one type of job that would not have been included in the employment advertisements ten years ago. List that job and explain why it was not available ten years ago.

7. Identify at least one type of job that you do not think will be included in the employment advertisements 50 years in the future. List that job and explain why it will not be available 50 years from now.

For many years, newspapers' employment advertisements were separated into two groups: "Help Wanted—Male" and "Help Wanted—Female." In 1968, the United States Equal Employment Opportunity Commission (EEOC) declared that employment advertisements that specified the gender of job applicants are illegal.

8. Do you think that there are still types of jobs for which an employer should legally be able to require the job applicant be a male? Explain why or why not.

9. Do you think that there are still types of jobs for which an employer should legally be able to require that the job applicant be a female? Explain why or why not.

(continued)

The Want Ads- -

The EEOC has also ruled that employment advertisements cannot make references to the age of job applicants, such as "age 35 to 45 preferred."

10. Does an employment advertisement that seeks "recent college graduate" violate the EEOC's rule against describing the age of job applicants? Explain why or why not.

11. Does an employment advertisement that says "experienced only need apply" violate the EEOC's rule against describing the age of job applicants? Explain why or why not.

12. Does an employment advertisement that seeks "mature workers" violate the EEOC's rule against describing the age of job applicants? Explain why or why not.

The Ethics of the "Advertorial" -

AN *ADVERTORIAL* is an advertisement that does not look like an advertisement. Rather, it is designed to look like editorial content in a magazine or newspaper. Usually, advertisers design their advertorials. Sometimes, a magazine or newspaper's staff designs the advertorials that appear in a publication. If an advertorial occupies a full page or several pages, it is usually labeled "advertisement" or "advertorial."

However, there are numerous examples of subtle advertising in magazines. For example, a fashion essay in a magazine may show models wearing fancy clothes. The copy below the photographs tells readers what brand of shoes, pants, belt, shirt, and makeup the models are wearing. In another magazine article, a celebrity may be shown in his attractive penthouse apartment. The copy may tell us what brand of carpet he has, as well as the brand of the sofa, draperies, and other furnishings. Even "self-improvement" articles may contain advertising. To help readers relax, a magazine may recommend certain musicians' mellow CDs. The article may suggest that the reader drink a soothing cup of a particular brand of herbal tea. A recently published book by a well-known psychologist may also be recommended.

Answer the following questions. Use another sheet of paper, if necessary.

1. Look through several magazines that you read regularly, or at least occasionally. Find three examples of editorial content that contains advertising within three different editorial articles. List the name of each article and describe the advertising.

   -

   -

   -

2. Most magazines are already full of advertisements. Explain why you think many magazine editors also include advertising within editorial content.

(continued)

The Ethics of the "Advertorial" -------------------

As discussed in Activity 2 in Unit 3, *ethics* are a set of moral principles. To be *ethical* is to do that which is morally correct under the circumstances.

3. Do you think advertorials that are labeled "advertising" or "advertorial" are ethical? Explain why or why not.

4. Do you think advertorials that are *not* labeled "advertising" or "advertorial" are ethical? Explain why or why not.

The American Society of Magazine Editors' Code of Ethics requires advertorials to be labeled "advertisement" or "advertorial." However, if a magazine fails to include this label, there is no penalty imposed.

5. If the Society cannot punish its members who violate the Society's Code of Ethics, why do you think that the Society even bothered to create a Code of Ethics? Explain your answer.

6. Should everything that is unethical also be illegal? Explain why or why not.

7. Is everything that is ethical also always legal? Explain why or why not.

(continued)

The Ethics of the "Advertorial" -

The next question is suggested as a group activity, as decided by your teacher.

8. Create a code of ethics for students at your school. You should create a numbered list of types of behavior that should be encouraged, as well as types of behavior that should be discouraged.

Code of Ethics for Students at _____

(name of your school)

1.

9. Do you normally follow the ethical code that you have created? Explain why or why not.

The objectives of this unit are to help students

- understand that technological change has an impact on social and economic change
- rely on their own creativity and imagination in generating new ideas for the future of print media
- develop their ability to make articulate and cogent written arguments
- anticipate Internet-driven changes in the future

A SUBSTANTIAL PARADIGM shift in the way newspapers and magazines present information has already begun. Many informed observers estimate that electronic forms of media will largely supplant paper and ink journalism by 2020. Most newspaper and magazine publishers are currently developing or improving electronic versions of their publications. Students have the opportunity in this unit to use critical and creative thinking to predict how newspapers and magazines will change, as well as predict how reading habits will shift.

In this Unit . . .

Newspapers Versus Magazines has students explore current trends in newspaper and magazine readership and asks students to predict future developments in media usage.

The Electronic Newspaper and Magazine encourages students to generate predictions about the emerging shift from printed to electronic journalism.

Freedom of the Press in a Changing World asks students to weigh freedom of the press within the context of increasingly complex national and international events.

What Happens Next? encourages students to use both analysis and creativity to make reasoned predictions about future news events.

Your Magazine has students rely on their creativity and imagination in a discussion about a hypothetical magazine of their own.

Paradigm Shifts introduces the concept of paradigm shifts and provides a pair of examples in the newspaper and magazine trades. Students then attempt to predict the next paradigm shift in these fields and write a five-paragraph persuasive essay supporting their prediction.

What Does a Journalist Need to Know? asks students to assess and rank the educational requirements for aspiring journalists. Students also examine their own interest in the field of journalism.

I believe very strongly that newspapers in their current, ink-on-paper form are an endangered species. As communications technologies evolve—and they *are* evolving at an *extraordinary* pace—newspapers are going to be subject to rapid and dramatic challenges in the marketplace.

William L. Winter (2000)
Former President, American Press Institute

I believe that the magazine format, as we understand it today, will survive for the next two decades, but printed editions will begin to give up ground to digital by 2010. The concept of magazines will change as technology evolves and as people become more comfortable with electronic reading.

Peter Meirs (2004)
Director of Alternative Media Technologies
Time Life Inc.

ALTHOUGH HUMANS have been using paper to communicate for over 5,000 years, paper's days may be numbered. One reason to question the future of paper is its effect on the environment. Paper comes from trees, and we must cut down trees to make paper and related products. After we are finished with a magazine or a newspaper, we dispose of it, creating solid waste. Electronic media do not require the clearing of forests, nor do electronic media load landfills with old paper. Of course, switching from paper to electronic media also affects the environment. This is because generating electricity uses natural resources such as coal and oil. This also causes air pollution.

> **In the future, it is likely that textbooks will also be available only in electronic form.**

Yet the switch from print media to electronic forms provides other benefits to society. Publishers will no longer have to pay to have their magazines and newspapers transported from the pressroom to consumers. This will reduce petroleum usage and air pollution from trucks and airplanes. The money saved on paper and transportation may benefit consumers in the form of lower prices for electronic versions of magazines and newspapers. We will also be able to receive updated news about important events almost instantaneously.

In the future, it is likely that textbooks will also be available only in electronic form. The computer software company Microsoft predicted that most magazines will be electronic by 2010, and that most paper publications will cease to exist by 2020. The printed book you are now reading may even become a collector's item someday.

In this unit, we will use the terms *newspapers* and *magazines* to include both their traditional printed versions and their new electronic versions.

Newspapers Versus Magazines -

BETWEEN 1993 and 2002, the number of daily newspapers in the United States declined from 1,556 to 1,457. During this same period, however, the number of American magazines increased from 14,302 to 17,254.

Answer the following questions. Use another sheet of paper, if necessary.

1. Why do you think the number of newspapers in the United States declined while the number of magazines increased? Explain your answer.

In 1994, there were 935 daily newspapers distributed in the evening and 635 distributed in the morning. Since then, many evening newspapers have shifted to morning distribution. In 2002, there were about 692 evening newspapers and 777 morning newspapers.

2. Newspaper publishers try to give their readers what they want. Why do you think many newspaper readers prefer morning newspapers to evening newspapers? Explain your answer.

In 2002, the average number of newspapers sold through subscription and retail sales during the week was about 55 million copies. Newspaper sales on Sundays increased to over 58 million.

3. Why do you think more people read the newspaper on Sunday than they do the rest of the week? Explain your answer.

Many magazines are trade magazines, which are magazines published for people in specific occupations, including photographers, lawyers, morticians, and hairstylists. Within occupations, there are specializations. For example, within the medical profession there are surgeons, ophthalmologists, pediatricians, oncologists, and so forth. All of these medical specializations have magazines written for them. Publishers produce consumer magazines based on people's interests rather than their occupations. Magazines such as *People* and *National Geographic* appeal to a wide variety of demographic and psychographic groups.

(continued)

Newspapers Versus Magazines - - - - - - - - - - - - - - - - -

4. Do you think there will be more trade magazines in the future than there are today? Explain why or why not.

5. Do you think there will be more consumer magazines in the future than there are today? Explain why or why not.

Because nearly all newspapers direct themselves toward particular communities, most readers choose their newspaper based on where they live. Readers select most magazines based on their interests rather than on where they live. As mentioned in the Buzz for Unit 3, the trend in magazines is away from general-interest magazines toward niches, or interests that are more specialized. The trend toward more specialized magazines reflects the trend among readers toward more specialized interests. This trend away from general interests bothers some sociologists and psychologists. (Sociologists are experts who study how societies behave; psychologists are experts who study how individuals behave.)

6. Why do you think that some sociologists and psychologists are worried about this trend toward more specialized interests among readers? Explain your answer.

7. Do you share their concern? Explain why or why not.

8. Do you think the trend toward more specialized magazines will continue in the future? Explain why or why not.

The Electronic Newspaper and Magazine - - - - - - - - - - - - - -

TODAY THERE ARE already many on-line magazines, such as salon.com and gurl.com. There are also many Internet versions of printed magazines and newspapers, such as time.com and chicagotribune.com. Many of these on-line publications are available to us on our desktop computers, laptop computers, digital phones, PDAs, and other electronic devices. In the near future, we will have computers that are no larger than a magazine. These computers will also weigh barely more than many magazines. The computer will operate on batteries, and will access the Internet through wireless transmission. The screens for these computers will be thin, flexible, and foldable, like paper. Engineers have already invented these devices. Their current challenge is to make this technology affordable to the average consumer.

Answer the following questions. Use another sheet of paper, if necessary.

1. Imagine that super-light, super-portable computers will be available to everybody within a year. You are the editor of a major magazine. How will you respond to this new technology? Explain your answer.

2. Some magazines have been more willing to add electronic versions than other magazines. What types of magazines have not been in a hurry to add electronic versions? Explain your answer.

3. What is one advantage that new technology will offer to the companies that advertise in newspapers and magazines? Explain your answer.

4. How will this new technology change our reading habits? Explain your answer.

5. As a consumer, are you looking forward to this change in how we read magazines and newspapers? Explain why or why not.

6. Think about the costs that newspaper and magazine publishers will save by switching from printed media to electronic media. Do you think that some newspapers and magazines will stop charging their readers for subscriptions? Explain why or why not.

Freedom of the Press in a Changing World - - - - - - - - - - - -

> The basis of our governments being the opinion of the people, the very first object should be to keep that right; and were it left to me to decide whether we should have a government without newspapers, or newspapers without a government, I should not hesitate a moment to prefer the latter.
>
> Thomas Jefferson, in a letter to Edward Carrington dated January 1787

Answer the following questions. Use another sheet of paper, if necessary.

1. Jefferson served as the third president of the United States. He says in the quotation above that, given the choice between a government without newspapers or newspapers without government, he would prefer newspapers without government. Do you agree with Jefferson? Explain why or why not.

> [T]o those who scare peace-loving people with phantoms of lost liberty, my message is this: Your tactics only aid terrorists, for they erode our national unity and diminish our resolve. They give ammunition to America's enemies, and pause to America's friends. They encourage people of goodwill to remain silent in the face of evil.
>
> United States Attorney General John Ashcroft, speaking to the Senate Judiciary Committee on December 6, 2001

Thomas Jefferson, who served as president of the United States from 1801 to 1809, and John Ashcroft, who served as attorney general of the United States from 2001 to 2005, lived in very different times. Jefferson's comments came during the period when the newly independent United States was writing its constitution. (The First Amendment, protecting freedom of the press, took effect in 1791.) Ashcroft's statement followed the tragic events of September 11, 2001.

2. Ashcroft said that people in the press who criticized the United States government were giving aid to our enemies. Do you agree? Explain why or why not.

3. When, if ever, do you think that it is okay for newspapers and magazines to print things that criticize our government? Explain your answer.

(continued)

Freedom of the Press in a Changing World----------

When Jefferson and other national leaders began creating the United States' national government, the idea of the "press" was unlike the press of today. There were very few magazines, most newspapers had only limited distribution, and electronic news media did not exist until more than 100 years later. The Internet arose nearly 200 years later. Today's press is much more complex and powerful than it was in Jefferson's day.

4. As the world becomes more complex, it becomes harder for the American government to deal with the United States' problems and problems in other parts of the world. Do you think Americans should be willing to give up part of their personal freedom (including some of the freedom of the press) in order to give the United States government more power to deal with these problems? Explain why or why not.

5. Ask an older adult the same question as question 4. Write their answer below.

6. Do you think freedom of the press will increase in the future, decrease, or stay about the same as today? Explain.

7. Ask an older adult the same question as question 6. Write their answer below.

8. Compare your answers to questions 4 and 6 with the older adult's answers to questions 5 and 7. Describe what you discover.

What Happens Next? -

NEWSPAPERS TRY to be as current as possible. After all, their job is to tell us "the news." However, most news articles do not try to predict the future. If they did, they would not be **objective**—they would be giving us opinions rather than facts. You, however, are not limited to just the facts. In this activity, you will try to predict the future.

Answer the following questions. Use another sheet of paper, if necessary.

Look through a recent newspaper (one published within the last two or three days). Find three news stories (not feature stories or opinion columns) that discuss current events in which you have some interest. For each of the three stories, describe the current situation, predict the future situation, and explain your prediction.

News story 1

Subject:

Current situation:

Your prediction of the future situation:

Your reasoning that supports your prediction:

(continued)

What Happens Next? -

News story 2

Subject:

Current situation:

Your prediction of the future situation:

Your reasoning that supports your prediction:

News story 3

Subject:

Current situation:

Your prediction of the future situation:

Your reasoning that supports your prediction:

Your Magazine

IMAGINE THAT YOU WORK for a major magazine publisher such as Time Warner. You are in charge of creating a new magazine that will appeal to as many teenagers as possible. This magazine will be available in print and on-line versions, and it will be distributed weekly.

Answer the following questions. Use another sheet of paper, if necessary.

1. What will be the name of your new magazine?

   • Explain why you chose this name.

2. What types of topics would you discuss each week? List and describe four.

   • Topic 1:

   Description:

   Why this topic is popular with teenagers:

   • Topic 2:

   Description:

   Why this topic is popular with teenagers:

   • Topic 3:

   Description:

   Why this topic is popular with teenagers:

   • Topic 4:

   Description:

   Why this topic is popular with teenagers:

(continued)

Your Magazine -

3. The cover of a magazine helps sell the magazine at newsstands and other stores. The company wants to use a photograph on the magazine's cover each week. What types of people or things would you put on the cover? List and explain three. (Instead of identifying particular people, identify *types* of people.)

- Magazine cover 1:

  Why this type of person/thing is popular with teenagers:

- Magazine cover 2:

  Why this type of person/thing is popular with teenagers:

- Magazine cover 3:

  Why this type of person/thing is popular with teenagers:

4. Which types of companies do you think would be interested in advertising in your magazine? (Remember, advertisers normally choose which magazines to advertise in, not vice versa.) List and explain three.

- Advertiser 1:

  Why this advertiser would want to advertise in your magazine:

- Advertiser 2:

  Why this advertiser would want to advertise in your magazine:

- Advertiser 3:

  Why this advertiser would want to advertise in your magazine:

Paradigm Shifts -

A *PARADIGM* is a commonly accepted way of doing something. For example, a paradigm in daily newspapers is that the weather forecast appears on the front page. Sometimes a paradigm changes. This is called a *paradigm shift.* Just one person, one event, or one publication may cause this shift. The current change from print media to electronic media represents a significant paradigm shift for newspaper and magazine publishers. However, there have been earlier paradigm shifts that changed the way newspapers and magazines presented information.

The Gannett newspaper chain founded *USA Today* in 1982. The idea of a national newspaper was uncommon. Although the *Wall Street Journal* and *The New York Times* have national distribution, both newspapers focus on specific events and places. *USA Today* presented a wider assortment of articles on events in which most Americans would be interested. *USA Today* was also the first American newspaper to use color photography and graphics on a daily basis. Its articles tended to be shorter than those in most other newspapers. Originally, *USA Today* avoided the use of **jumps,** and printed entire articles, no matter how important, on only one page. The newspaper also relied on the frequent use of charts and graphs to present information. One of the most dramatic uses of colored graphics was *USA Today*'s weather map; many other newspapers have since adopted similar ways of presenting weather information. Today, after many years of losing money, *USA Today* has become profitable and has the largest newspaper circulation in the United States, distributing more than 2 million copies daily.

This activity discusses two paradigm shifts. In 1982, *USA Today* started a major shift in the way printed newspapers presented information. Today, newspapers and magazines are involved in a paradigm shift from print media to electronic media.

Answer the following questions. Use another sheet of paper, if necessary.

1. Presume that it is now the year 2020. Newspapers and magazines have completed their shift to electronic media. Most of us now walk around with our wireless electronic computers that are no larger nor heavier than the printed publications of the past. What will be the *next* paradigm shift for newspapers and magazines? Write a five-paragraph persuasive essay that provides three good reasons why your prediction for the next paradigm shift is a valid one.

Before you get started, think about the following:

- Many people try to predict future important trends in media. For example, people in the recorded-music industry predicted that most teenagers would continue to buy CDs instead of downloading music. They were wrong!

(continued)

Paradigm Shifts -

- Even corporate and government leaders often guess incorrectly when trying to anticipate paradigm shifts. Some wait too long to adjust. (These include the typewriter manufacturers that went bankrupt when people shifted from typewriters to word-processing computers.) Others introduce new ideas that the public ignores or resists. (In 1990, a publisher introduced the first and still only daily national sports newspaper, *The National Sports Daily*. It failed in less than two years.)

- Most teenagers are experts on current trends. Use your imagination when trying to identify a future trend!

The Five-Paragraph Persuasive Essay

I. Introductory Paragraph with Thesis Statement

The thesis is the argument that you are trying to persuade the reader to agree with. In this case, your thesis is simple: you are going to tell the reader what the next important paradigm shift will be in the newspaper and magazine industries after they have moved to electronic media. In the introductory paragraph, you will also list the three pieces of evidence that you will use in the body of the essay. In this case, your evidence is your three reasons why your prediction is a good one.

II. Body: First Piece of Evidence

It is best to analyze your three pieces of evidence and evaluate how strong each argument is, then rank them 1, 2, 3. Because you want to have a strong finish, many people recommend saving the strongest argument for last. However, because you do not want to get off to a bad start, begin the body of the essay with your second-strongest argument. In this way, you can "hide" your weakest argument in the middle. Make certain that you have a transition between each argument. Each of the paragraphs of the body should lead into the next paragraph.

III. Body: Second Piece of Evidence

Present your weakest argument.

IV. Body: Third Piece of Evidence

Present your strongest argument.

V. Conclusion

Restate your thesis, and include the three points you have used to prove that thesis.

What Does a Journalist Need to Know? - - - - - - - - - - - - - - - -

MANY PEOPLE CREDIT New York's Columbia University as the first college to create a program to educate professional journalists. This occurred about a hundred years ago. At the time, "journalism" meant creating and writing newspapers and magazines. Today, journalism includes electronic media such as television, radio, and the Internet. As technology has changed over the past century, journalism education has also changed. In the future, journalism and the training of people who want to be journalists will continue to change.

A typical college degree requires about forty courses. General education courses are required for all students, no matter what program they are studying. These may number about twenty courses, or half the total courses required. For this activity, we will presume that a student majoring in journalism at M.B.U. (Make Believe University) needs to take twenty journalism courses and twenty general education courses to graduate. We will not worry about the highly specialized journalism courses. Instead, we will focus on the general education courses.

Answer the following questions. Use another sheet of paper, if necessary.

1. Rate the importance of the following courses for journalism students, circling your answer for each.

	Not Important			Very Important	
Math	1	2	3	4	5
Writing	1	2	3	4	5
Literature	1	2	3	4	5
Geography	1	2	3	4	5
Foreign Language	1	2	3	4	5
American History	1	2	3	4	5
World History	1	2	3	4	5
Art Appreciation	1	2	3	4	5
Music Appreciation	1	2	3	4	5
Speech	1	2	3	4	5
Government (Civics)	1	2	3	4	5

(continued)

What Does a Journalist Need to Know?- - - - - - - - - - - -

	Not Important			Very Important	
Chemistry	1	2	3	4	5
Biology	1	2	3	4	5
Psychology (the study of how individuals behave)	1	2	3	4	5
Sociology (the study of how groups of people behave)	1	2	3	4	5
Physical Education	1	2	3	4	5
Business and Economics	1	2	3	4	5
Law	1	2	3	4	5

Choose three of the courses that you rated the most important, and explain why you believe each is more important than the other courses.

2. Course name:

   Why more important:

3. Course name:

   Why more important:

4. Course name:

   Why more important:

(continued)

What Does a Journalist Need to Know?-------------

Now choose three of the courses that you rated the least important, and explain why you believe each is less important than the other courses.

5. Course name:

    Why not as important:

6. Course name:

    Why not as important:

7. Course name:

    Why not as important:

8. Are there any general education subjects that you think are important for journalism students to take but that are not on the list above? Explain why or why not.

9. Newspapers and magazines often assign journalists to parts of the world that are dangerous. The danger may be due to warfare, crime, natural disasters, bad weather, or disease. Do you think you would personally find these types of assignments exciting, scary, or both? Explain your answer.

10. Do you think you would like to be a journalist? Explain why or why not.

Glossary

caption—a statement in a newspaper or magazine that describes the subject matter of a photograph that appears in the publication

circulation—the average number of copies of a publication sold or distributed over a given period. That period is based on how frequently a publication is issued—daily, weekly, monthly, and so forth.

data mining—the practice used by publishers and advertisers in which they use **demographics** and **psychographics** gathered about consumers to make publishing and advertising decisions

demographics—statistics about people grouped by such information as age, gender, ethnicity, geography, and income. For example, we know that the demographic group that is most likely to read *Cosmopolitan* is women.

feature story—an article that discusses information that is of interest to readers, but is not considered "news." Examples of feature stories include biographical sketches of interesting people, fashion articles, and articles that provide tips on managing people's day-to-day responsibilities.

jump—the term for when a magazine or newspaper article continues on, or jumps to, another page

news service—an organization that collects and assembles the news to be used by newspapers and other news agencies. Among the most important English language news services are the Associated Press and Reuters. News services are often called "wire services," because they transmit information to thousands of news agencies electronically.

objective—based on facts, without personal opinions or interpretation (the opposite of subjective)

psychographics—people grouped by their interests, attitudes, values, and habits (including buying habits). For example, the psychographic group that is most likely to read *American Hunter* is people interested in guns and hunting.

sensationalism—a writing style that intentionally attempts to play on readers' emotions (anger, sentimentality, and so forth) rather than relying on simple explanation of facts

synergy—coordinated interaction between two or more organizations, designed to create a combined effect that is greater than the results those organizations could have each had on their own. For example, if *ESPN the Magazine* encourages its readers to watch ESPN, and ESPN television encourages its viewers to read *ESPN the Magazine,* the magazine is helping the television network to make more money, and vice versa.

target market—the **demographic** or **psychographic** group that publishers and advertisers want to reach. To reach this target market, publishers will tailor their articles to attract that group.

wire service—See **news service**

Additional Resources

Books

Bosmajian, Haig A., ed., *The Freedom to Publish* (New York: Neal-Schuman, 1989).

Carter, Robert A., and S. William Pattis, *Opportunities in Publishing Careers* (Lincolnwood, IL: VGM Career Books, 2001).

Currie, Dawn H., *Girl Talk: Adolescent Magazines and Their Readers* (Toronto: University of Toronto, 1999).

Farish, Leah, *The First Amendment: Freedom of Speech, Religion, and the Press* (Springfield, NJ: Enslow, 1998).

Levy, Beth, and Denise M. Bonilla, eds., *The Power of the Press* (New York: H.W. Wilson, 1999).

Petley, Julian, *Media: The Impact on Our Lives* (Austin, TX: Raintree, 2001.)

Roberts, Donald F., and Ulla G. Foehr, *Kids and Media in America* (New York: Cambridge University, 2004).

Starkey, Carolyn Morton, and Norgina Wright Penn, *What You Need to Know About Reading Labels, Directions, and Newspapers* (Lincolnwood, IL: National Textbook, 1994).

Web Sites

Magazine Publishers of America
www.magazine.org

Media Post
www.mediapost.com

New York Times Student Connection
www.nytimes.com/learning/students/index.html

Newspaper Association of America
www.naa.org

Newspapers in Education Online
www.nieonline.com

Student Press Law Center
www.splc.org

Teen Ink
www.teenink.com

Who Owns What
www.cjr.org/tools/owners/

Share Your Bright Ideas

We want to hear from you!

Your name_____Date_____

School name_____

School address_____

City _____State _____Zip_____Phone number (_____)_____

Grade level(s) taught_____Subject area(s) taught_____

Where did you purchase this publication?_____

In what month do you purchase a majority of your supplements?_____

What moneys were used to purchase this product?

____School supplemental budget ____Federal/state funding ____Personal

Please "grade" this Walch publication in the following areas:

	A	B	C	D
Quality of service you received when purchasing	A	B	C	D
Ease of use	A	B	C	D
Quality of content	A	B	C	D
Page layout	A	B	C	D
Organization of material	A	B	C	D
Suitability for grade level	A	B	C	D
Instructional value	A	B	C	D

COMMENTS:_____

_____

What specific supplemental materials would help you meet your current—or future—instructional needs?

_____

Have you used other Walch publications? If so, which ones?_____

May we use your comments in upcoming communications? ____Yes ____No

Please **FAX** this completed form to **888-991-5755**, or mail it to

Customer Service, Walch Publishing, P. O. Box 658, Portland, ME 04104-0658

We will send you a **FREE GIFT** in appreciation of your feedback. **THANK YOU!**